CREATIVE BIBLE LESSONS
ON THE TRINITY

12 SESSIONS TO HELP STUDENTS
UNDERSTAND THEIR PLACE IN GOD'S STORY
PERFECT FOR SUNDAY SCHOOL, YOUTH MEETINGS, SMALL GROUPS, AND MORE!

ANDREW HEDGES

ZONDERVAN®

ZONDERVAN.com/
AUTHORTRACKER
follow your favorite authors

youth specialties

ZONDERVAN

Creative Bible Lessons on the Trinity
Copyright © 2012 by Andrew Hedges

YS Youth Specialties is a trademark of YOUTHWORKS!, INCORPORATED and is registered with the United States Patent and Trademark Office.

This title is also available as a Zondervan ebook. Visit www.zondervan.com/ebooks.

Requests for information should be addressed to:

Zondervan, 5300 *Patterson Ave. SE, Grand Rapids, Michigan* 49530

Library of Congress Cataloging-in-Publication Data

Hedges, Andrew A., 1977-
    Creative Bible lessons on the Trinity : 12 sessions to help students understand their place in God's story : perfect for Sunday School, youth meetings, small groups, and more! / Andrew Hedges.
      p. cm.
    Includes bibliographical references (pp. 155—156).
    ISBN 978-0-310-67119-0 (softcover)
    1. Trinity—Study and teaching. 2. Christian education of teenagers. I. Title.
BT111.3.H43 2012
231'.0440712—dc23
                                                       2011045989

Cover design: SharpSeven Design
Interior design: Matthew Van Zomeren

Printed in the United States of America

12 13 14 15 16 17 18 /DCI/ 22 21 20 19 18 17 16 15 14 13 12 11 10 9 8 7 6 5 4 3 2 1

DEDICATION

To our one and only God—Father, Son, and Spirit. You are all our hope and peace.

ACKNOWLEDGMENTS

Many thanks to . . .

The members of the publishing team: Greg Clouse, Jeremy Jones, Matt Gilson, Janelle DeBlaay, Janie Wilkerson, and Ben Fetterley.

An incredible church staff—Shirley Wilkerson, Mark Simpson, Wade Harris—and my brother, Aaron, for the friendship and insights.

My three princesses: Anna, Ella, and Abby. Thanks for lighting up my days! God uses you to encourage me and remind me of his presence.

Cara, my gift. God has and continues to love me through you and gives me a glimpse of heaven.

CONTENTS

PREFACE
THE TRINITY AND TEENS

We are human; therefore we value relationship. It's as if we were wired for it from the beginning of time. We are miserable in isolation. All we ever seem to want is to feel like we belong. It doesn't matter whether we are children, adults, or teenagers. We value relationship. We crave it. We need it.

When we consider who God is, we begin to understand why we value relationship. We actually *have* been wired this way from the beginning of time. If we were created in the image of God, then God himself must be a relationship. British theologian Alister McGrath puts it this way: "When you are explaining what Christianity is all about to your interested friends, you needn't mention the word *Trinity* at all. You speak to them about God, and about the way in which God has revealed himself to us and reconciled us to himself through Jesus Christ. But if you were to sit down and start thinking about the question 'What must God be like if he is able to act in this way?' you will end up with the doctrine of the Trinity."[1]

[1] Alister E. McGrath, *Understanding the Trinity* (England: Kingsway Publications, Ltd., 1988), 115.

God exists as a Trinity—Father, Son, Spirit—equal in nature yet distinct in expression. The very nature of God is relational, and the very heart of God is for relationship.

In our churches we sometimes promote critical study (knowing about) over relationship (knowing). Yet at the heart of Christianity is a relationship—one of knowing and being known by God. We can and should begin with Jesus, but our thoughts and discussions eventually should go deeper. For many teens going deeper raises many doubts and fears that they desperately need to work through in order to be truly rooted and established in the love of God.

The passion behind this book is to move beyond a superficial understanding of a relationship with God without losing the intensity of the relationship. The more clarity we have in how God himself exists in relationship or community, the better our understanding of his desire and our need for a relationship with him. We may have doubts and fears, but our deep relationship with our triune God will see us through.

My intent in writing this book is to have it flow like a conversation. With each session teens should learn more about God and more about themselves. As the story of God unfolds, so does our story. Perhaps a helpful overview would sound something like this: The God who is three-in-one (Session 1) has spoken and revealed his desire to have a relationship with us (Session 2), and he has initiated a plan to make that happen (Session 3). God himself miraculously came to earth (Session 4) to live as a perfect human (Session 5), die in our place (Session 6), and be raised from the dead (Session 7) to give us hope that we can be in a relationship with him as part of his family (Session 8). As he works in our lives, we are changed more and more into his image (Session 9) and begin to look like him (Session 10) and live like him (Session 11) as the representation of his heart and mission for the world (Session 12).

Of all our relationships, the one we have with God the Father through Jesus Christ in the power of the Holy Spirit is the most amazing gift we could ever hope to receive. Teens may understand this whether they know God or not. All humanity has a desire for intimacy, and teens are in a developmental stage of heightened social awareness and longing for belonging. We all can find true satisfaction in a relationship with our Creator. And if this is true, then it leads us to the questions: What must God be like if we who are created in his image are so wired toward relationships? What does it mean for us that our God is so relationally defined in his very essence? Use this book to introduce your teens to the God who is three-in-one.

Praise to the Father, Son, and Spirit,

Andrew A. Hedges

INTRODUCTION
MAKING THE MOST OF THIS STUDY

PHILOSOPHY: LEARNING HOW YOUR TEENS LEARN

In order to understand how to most effectively use this book, it's important for you to know the teaching philosophy behind it. In the same way, in order to teach your students effectively, you need to know how they learn. In her book *Learning Styles: Reaching Everyone God Gave You to Teach*, education specialist Marlene LeFever provides insight into how people learn. For the purpose of understanding the book in your hands, the following paragraphs from LeFever's book will provide a basic understanding of the terms. (Note: The icon that appears next to each description will be used throughout this book to designate activities that fit that particular learning style.)

IMAGINATIVE LEARNER

Imaginative Learners are feeling people who get involved with others and learn best in settings that allow interpersonal relationships to develop. These curious, questioning learners learn by listening and sharing ideas. They see the broad overview or big picture much more easily than the small details. They learn by sensing, feeling, watching. They can see all sides of the issues presented.

ANALYTIC LEARNER

Analytic Learners learn by watching and listening. They expect a teacher to be the primary information giver, while they sit and carefully assess the value of the information presented. These are the students who learn in the way most teachers have traditionally taught, and so they are often considered the best learners. They are strategic planners, and they aim for perfection—the right answers, the As in school and in life. These learners want all the data before they make a decision.

COMMON SENSE LEARNER

Common Sense Learners like to play with ideas to see if they are rational and workable. These students want to test theory in the real world, to apply what has been learned. They love to get the job done. They are hands-on people who, using their own ideas, can analyze problems and solve or fix them. Common Sense Learners, as the name suggests, excel when dealing with what is practical and of immediate importance to them. They learn best when learning is combined with doing.

DYNAMIC LEARNER

Dynamic Learners also enjoy action as part of the learning process, but rather than thinking projects through to their rational conclusion, Dynamic Learners excel in following hunches and sensing new directions and possibilities. These risk takers thrive on situations that call for flexibility and change and find real joy in starting something new or putting their personal stamp of originality on an idea."[2]

God has made each of us wonderfully unique, including the way we learn. These four basic learning styles provide only a glimpse of how students learn during any given lesson. Within each learning style you will also find students who learn best through various types of activities, including **auditory** (hearing) 🧠, **visual** (seeing) 👁, or **tactile/kinesthetic** (feeling/doing) ✋. You may have an Imaginative Learner who seems to respond more to pictures or videos. One Common Sense Learner may fit into a more tactile/kinesthetic, or hands-on, style, while another prefers to sit and listen to a recording or guest lecturer. Each student has a different combination by which he or she learns best.

As you use this curriculum, the best place to start is yourself. Take time to read over the learning styles again, and then consider whether you're more auditory, visual, or tactile/kinesthetic. Which description fits you best? There's no wrong answer. Just keep in mind that most teachers teach the way they learn best. But recognizing your own style will help you concentrate on reaching *all* the learning styles found within your group of students.

For your benefit this curriculum has been designed to reach all four learning styles in each session. In the next section we'll take a look at how you can use this book to reach each one God has given you to teach.

METHODOLOGY: HOW TO USE THIS BOOK

Another goal of this book is to help you teach these truths about God without your teens feeling as though they're being

[2] Marlene LeFever. *Learning Styles: Reaching Everyone God Gave You to Teach.* (Colorado Springs, Colo.: David C. Cook Publishing Co., 1995), 21.

taught. Hopefully, you and your teens will find this curriculum to hold a much more conversational tone than the average study. The idea is to create a sense of dialogue about the persons and work of the Trinity throughout each session. The goal is to lead teens to an understanding of the Trinity on their own—instead of telling them what to believe.

With these things in mind, each of the learning activities is labeled in order to help you see which style and preference is strongest for each activity. However, some of the learning activities may cross or combine several styles and preferences. The idea is to work out the best scenario for your particular group.

In each session you'll find boldface text for content that's meant to be spoken or read aloud to the group. You're welcome to read it word for word or to summarize. At the very least, take the bold font as a signal for you to address the group.

Also note that along with the reproducible small-group worksheets at the end of each session, there are leader's worksheets that provide you with sample responses and insights into the issues each question may raise. These aren't designed as comprehensive answer sheets, but as a support for you as you lead group discussion.

Following is a brief explanation of each part of the sessions:

OVERVIEW

We hope these learning objectives are realized throughout your conversation with the teens.

SETTING THE TONE

Here you'll find a short section with some personal thoughts to help get your mind working through the concepts you'll be discussing with your teens.

BREAKING THE ICE

Every conversation needs an icebreaker. The Imaginative Learners will take the lead of these activities as they get excited about talking things out. You'll get their side of the conversation going from the start.

TRANSITIONAL TRUTH

These are Scripture-guided insights through which your side of the dialogue will help keep the lesson flowing from one concept to another. You can use these as a framework for how you'll share your heart and thoughts with your group, or you can read this text directly.

HEARING THE WORD

These are primarily small-group or pairing activities during which teens will search God's Word and learn more about the persons and work of the Trinity. They'll also allow you to hear how your teens are interpreting what they're reading.

SHARING YOUR PERSPECTIVE

These activities will be great opportunities to get your Common Sense Learners talking about their concept of the Trinity and how it plays out in their everyday thinking and living.

MAKING IT PERSONAL

While other parts may appear in a variety of places in each lesson, we'll always land on a place where students can personalize what they've learned. The Dynamic Learners can run with this segment. It provides an opportunity to show where the theme of the lesson can go after the study time is over and consider thoughts for further personal reflection.

BRINGING IT TOGETHER

This section will summarize what's been learned and recap the journey to this point. There will be opportunities to review a basic concept from past sessions in order to keep things fresh in teens' minds. Each concept builds upon another, so we can't feel done when we've completed the lesson but rather one step closer to our understanding of the Trinity.

One final note about the sections concerns the timing. The length of each lesson will differ according to the size of your group and the amount of time you decide to dedicate to each part. Generally speaking, the lessons are designed for a one-hour time frame. However, other learning activities can easily be added to fill any additional time. The more time you use, the more opportunities your teens will have to learn within their respective learning styles and preferences. The choice is yours!

THE TRIUNITY OF GOD
SESSION ONE

OVERVIEW

This lesson provides a definition of the Trinity. Teens will look at Bible passages relating to the equality and distinction of the persons of the Godhead, understand what each means regarding relationship within the Trinity, and reflect on this sense of community as it relates to teens' personal lives.

SETTING THE TONE

Community lies at the heart of the Trinity. The Father, Son, and Spirit share the highest and most perfect expression of what it means to live in unity and harmony. God commands that his church exhibit these characteristics (Romans 15:5-6). As believers do this, they faithfully portray the heart of God himself.

If we seek to create a community based only on human ideas, it will inevitably end up in a mess. Still, our hearts and minds constantly try to create community that revolves around ourselves. Teens sense this tension in their everyday community settings, including family, school, teams, clubs, church, and others. It's essential that we try to model our lives after the one perfect expression of community—the heart of our triune God.

BREAKING THE ICE
(7-8 MINUTES)

OPTION 1: A JOYFUL NOISE?

Ask two members of your group to sing out loud on your signal. Tell each of them to sing a different song, but don't let the other know. Then cue the music, and let 'em go! The time limit is as much as you can bear.

Next have two other teens (or the same ones) sing a song together—one singing melody and the other harmony. When you've heard the difference, take some time to discuss.

QUESTIONS TO ASK

1. What's the difference between the two singing sessions?
2. If God is three-in-one, then what kind of God would he be if the three persons sang a different song?
3. How does singing in harmony add to the beauty or understanding of the music? How do you think this relates to God?

OPTION 2: THE POWER OF UNITY

Before you play the short video *The Power of Unity* from Worship House Media, say something like—

> **This clip focuses on unity among Christians, but it gives us a glimpse of what a true community looks like. Take a look, and think about how this look at unity is like or unlike the Trinity.**

After you play the clip, take some time to discuss a few questions.

QUESTIONS TO ASK

1. **How do you think this blend relates to believers in the church?**
2. **What does this kind of diversity and unity say about God?**
3. **In what ways do you think the relationship of the Father, Son, and Spirit are similar to the way unity was presented in this video?**

TRANSITIONAL TRUTH

Say—

> **In Deuteronomy 6:4 the Bible says, "Hear, O Israel: The LORD our God, the LORD is one." This statement "the LORD is one" means two things. First, God is the one-and-only God. Second, God is one in himself. But how can God be one if we also believe the Son and Spirit are God? Let's take a look at a few passages that might help us better see what the Bible teaches about the Trinity.**

3. *The Power of Unity* directed by Church Fuel. Worship House Media, www.worshiphousemedia.com/mini-movies/6408/The-Power-Of-Unity.

HEARING THE WORD
(10-15 MINUTES)

SAME, NOT THE SAME

Have the teens arrange into small groups; you can determine the numbers to fit your needs. Hand each one a copy of the **Same, Not the Same worksheet** found at the end of this session. Give each group time to answer the questions. You may want to assign one or two questions to each group, so they can be more thorough in the answers. When most groups have finished, have each one share the answers with the rest of the class.

TRANSITIONAL TRUTH

So God being three in one makes us ask, "How can this be?" We can see God listed as Father, Son, and Spirit (three persons), and there are Bible passages that show each one is fully God himself. Is there an easy way for us to explain this? Let's take some time to share some perspectives on this. What do you think?

SHARING YOUR PERSPECTIVE
(12-15 MINUTES)

WALK IT OUT

Use the **Walk It Out leader's worksheet** at the end of this session to read through the descriptions of the Trinity. Then assign each corner of the room a different description, and read through it once more. Have the teens stand and move to

YOU'LL NEED

- Copies of the **Same, Not the Same worksheet**
- Pens or pencils
- Bibles

the corner of the room that represents the perspective they believe makes the most sense in explaining the Trinity. When they've made their choices, either have them stay or bring everyone back together to give the titles of each description and the problems with each perspective.

TRANSITIONAL TRUTH

Now that we have a clear definition of the Trinity, let's consider the awesome relationship that exists among the three persons and what that tells us about our lives in community with God and each another.

MAKING IT PERSONAL
(15-20 MINUTES)

IT'S IN THE BAG!

Ask the teens to pair up for a three-legged race. Pass out potato sacks or ties to connect them. After their legs are together, each person should also put an arm around the other's shoulder. At this point they will collectively have only two arms (each person's outside arm) available. Give each pair an inflated balloon. The goal of each pair is to make it across the room to a chair where one person will hold the balloon steady while the other member of the pair sits and breaks the balloon. The first pair to make it back to the starting line wins!

QUESTIONS TO ASK:

1. **What are the different ways each of you worked in your pairs? What was the same?**
2. **How does this relate to the unity (oneness) and harmony (togetherness) of God?**
3. **How can we express this unity and harmony in our group or church as we try to give others a picture of our great God?**

> **YOU'LL NEED**
> - Potato sacks, bags, or ties
> - Balloons
> - Prizes for winners

BRINGING IT TOGETHER

Finish with something along these lines—

> Each session of this study will continue to show how the persons of the Trinity work together in unity and harmony to reveal God to us, gift us with eternal salvation, and equip us to be followers of Jesus. Let's pray for ourselves and each other as we grow and experience God together.

Pray this or something similar—

> Great God, we know you're awesome and beyond what we can imagine. But you still want to have a relationship with us and have chosen to make yourself known to us. Thank you for who you are and what you do in our lives. Help us to reflect you in our personal lives and as a community. Father, we ask this through your Son and in the power of the Spirit—one God, forever and ever. Amen.

SESSION 1:
THE TRIUNITY OF GOD

SAME, NOT THE SAME
SMALL-GROUP WORKSHEET

1. Read Deuteronomy 4:32-39. Why does God say that the miracles, wonders, and words of God were given to the people?

2. What does the Bible teach that God says about proclaiming someone or something else to be a god (see Isaiah 42:8; 48:11)? What does the apostle Paul say about idols and God (see 1 Corinthians 8:4-6)?

3. How does Jesus refer to himself in John 5:25, 10:36, and 11:4? What difference does it make that Jesus was accused of *blasphemy* (a crime of assuming the rights or qualities of God)?

4. Read Acts 5:1-11. Why did Peter treat Ananias and Sapphira so seriously? How is the Holy Spirit regarded in terms of God?

5. How do you think a God who is three distinct persons—Father, Son, Spirit—shows unity and harmony?

SESSION 1:
THE TRIUNITY OF GOD

SAME, NOT THE SAME
LEADER'S WORKSHEET

1. Read Deuteronomy 4:32-39. Why does God say that the miracles, wonders, and words of God were given to the people?
   The focus of verses 35 and 39 is that there is only one God and no other beside him.

2. What does the Bible teach that God says about proclaiming someone or something else to be a god (see Isaiah 42:8; 48:11)? What does the apostle Paul say about idols and God (see 1 Corinthians 8:4-6)?
   God does not give up any of his glory, praise, or divine name to any idol or anyone who might claim to be a god. He defends and protects his name. Paul says that no matter how many so-called gods there are, there is only one God who gives us life and whom we worship. Paul also includes Jesus in his discussion, saying that he is our source of life.

3. How does Jesus refer to himself in John 5:25, 10:36, and 11:4? What difference does it make that Jesus was accused of *blasphemy* (a crime of assuming the rights or qualities of God)?
   Jesus consistently calls himself the Son of God. He further claims the power to give life (John 5:25) and says that God would glorify the Son (John 11:4). This would have been absolutely offensive to the Jewish leaders who held to a strict monotheistic view that God was the only God.

4. Read Acts 5:1-11. Why did Peter treat Ananias and Sapphira so seriously? How is the Holy Spirit regarded in terms of God?
   This couple wasn't simply lying to Peter. They were lying before God about what they were giving. A lie to the Holy Spirit (v. 3) is a lie against God (v. 4).

5. How do you think a God who is three distinct persons—Father, Son, Spirit—shows unity and harmony?
   This question is meant to prompt some ideas that should be discussed as this lesson and series progress. Some sample responses might include the following: "They think the same way," "They work together to accomplish a task," or, "They can't possibly work together if they are three different people."

SESSION 1:
THE TRIUNITY OF GOD

WALK IT OUT
LEADER'S WORKSHEET

Read each of these different ways of understanding the Trinity, but don't name the titles until your teens have chosen their perspective and its corresponding corner of the room. You can use the italicized information that follows each explanation to help with the follow-up discussion.

1. MODALISM (ALSO SABELLIANISM)[4]

God is not really three distinct persons, but only one person who appears to people in different modes at different times. In other words, God appears as the Father at some times, as the Son at others, and as the Spirit at others.

This view follows John 10:30 where Jesus says, "I and the Father are one." However, it denies the Bible's examples of God as three persons, such as the baptism of Jesus in Luke 3:21-22. If God simply changes mode or form each time, then the baptism of Jesus couldn't have happened the way the Bible says.

2. ARIANISM

God the Son was at one point created by God the Father. Before that time the Son and Holy Spirit didn't exist—only the Father. Therefore, the Father is the only God, and Jesus is a supreme being who is like God but not God himself. If this is true of Jesus, then it's also true of the Holy Spirit.

*This view follows John 3:16 when Jesus calls himself "only begotten Son" (KJV). But begotten doesn't need to mean that Jesus was created. The Arian view also doesn't take into account the Bible passages provided in the **Same, Not the Same** worksheet stating that each person—Father, Son, and Spirit—is God. So it denies that each person is fully God. If Jesus wasn't God, then he wasn't perfect. If he wasn't perfect, then his death wouldn't have been enough for our salvation (more on this at a later session).*

[4.] The descriptions in this worksheet come from Wayne Grudem, *Systematic Theology* (Grand Rapids, Mich.: Zondervan, 1994) 226-248.

3. TRITHEISM

God is three persons, and each person is fully God. So there are three Gods.

This viewpoint denies the clearly stated teaching that there is only one God. It follows more of an ancient, pagan approach to the Trinity. There aren't really any current groups that hold to this position, but many Christians tend to lean this way in the way they speak about the Trinity or pray. For example, some believers pray to the Spirit for power but wouldn't think to direct a request like that to the Father or the Son. Yet all three persons are involved together in the giving of power to believers.

4. TRINITARIANISM

God eternally exists as three persons—Father, Son, and Holy Spirit. Each person is fully God, and there is one God. The three persons of God are distinct in their personal expressions but undivided in their divine nature.

In other words, there is only one God, and the one God is three. Each one has a specific way of expressing divinity, but each is equally and at the same time the one true God. This is the definition used in the writing and teaching of this study. It will continue to be expressed in the following lessons with the idea of bringing more clarity each time we approach it.

OVERVIEW

During this session teens will consider the power of the Father's Word, understand his role in providing direction, and decide to tune in to his voice.

SETTING THE TONE

You can get to know quite a bit about people by observing them over a period of time. You'd learn even more if you were to go through someone's house to look at pictures on the walls or how things are set up. But there's no better way to get to know people than by talking with them. Nothing can replace the power of the spoken word. Through conversation you might affirm some of the things you thought you knew about a person, or you may correct some of your misperceptions.

God saw fit to reveal himself in creation and personal experiences (those are extremely helpful) but also through his Word. The Trinity is one in divine nature, but we need to also understand how each person is distinct in his expression. God the Father reveals himself in the Word and through the Word (his Son) and has given us the Spirit to help us understand the Word. We can take hope in the fact that God desires to speak to us and wants to help us understand what he's saying.

BREAKING THE ICE
(8-10 MINUTES)

OPTION 1: THE LABORATORY

Give each member of your group paper and something to write with. Then begin your session by saying something like—

> **Tonight I'm going to ask you to get to know me better. In order to do this, you'll need to be a careful observer. Pretend you are a scientist in a laboratory who is writing a description of a new specimen. I'll just quietly be here for three or four minutes, and you can write your observations on your journal paper.**

While your group writes, feel free to make faces, move around the room, or break into a dance groove—just don't speak. The point is for them get to know you simply through observation. When the time is up, ask the following questions.

QUESTIONS TO ASK

1. **What are some of the things you observed about God?**
2. **How did they help you get to know God better?**

3. How do you know if your observations are correct?

4. What's the difference between knowing *about* someone and really *knowing* them?

5. What do you think is the best way to get to know God?

OPTION 2: THE OUTDOOR LABORATORY

Pass out paper and pencils to each member of your group, and take everyone outside. Then begin your session by saying something like—

> Tonight I'm going to ask you to get to know God better. In order to do this, you'll need to be a careful observer. Pretend you are a scientist in your outdoor laboratory who is writing a description of a new specimen. Use your senses to learn all you can about God for the next few minutes, and write your observations on your journal paper.

When the time is up, ask the following questions.

QUESTIONS TO ASK

1. What are some of the things you observed about God?

2. How did they help you get to know God better?

3. How do you know if your observations are correct?

4. What's the difference between knowing *about* someone and really *knowing* them?

5. What do you think is the best way to get to know God?

TRANSITIONAL TRUTH

Say something like—

> Hebrews 1:1-3 tells us, "In the past God spoke to our ancestors through the prophets at many times and in various ways, but in these last days he has spoken to us by his Son, whom he appointed heir of all things, and through whom also he made the universe. The Son is the radiance of God's glory and the exact representation of his being, sustaining all things by his powerful word."
>
> It's important for us to think through how God has spoken to us to reveal himself, especially through the Word. Let's take some time to consider this together.

HEARING THE WORD
10-12 MINUTES

WORD FOR WORD

YOU'LL NEED

• Copies of the **Word for Word worksheet**

• Bibles

• Paper

• Pens or pencils

Have the teens arrange into small groups; you can determine the numbers to fit your needs. Give each one a copy of the **Word for Word worksheet** found at the end of this session. Give each group time to answer the questions. You may want to assign one or two questions to each group, so they can be more thorough in the answers. When most groups have finished, have each one share the answers with the rest of the class.

TRANSITIONAL TRUTH

Say something like—

God has graciously given us more than clues or suggestions about who he is and what he wants for us. He has given us his Word. John 1:16-18 states, "Out of his fullness we have all received grace in place of grace already given. For the law was given through Moses; grace and truth came through Jesus Christ. No one has ever seen God, but the one and only Son, who is himself God and is in closest relationship with the Father, has made him known."

The Law was great, and Jesus was greater. Jesus perfectly showed us who God is and how God's Word is to be lived out every day.

SHARING YOUR PERSPECTIVE
(15-20 MINUTES)

TRYOUTS

Say something like—

The Father, Son, and Spirit show a complete unity in the Word, and harmony is the way the Word is revealed. That kind of unity and harmony is hard to achieve. Let's try to illustrate how those might work out in a few different situations.

Have your teens get into pairs or small groups. Ask each group to create a living illustration of how the Trinity works together to give, deliver, and reveal the Word of God. The challenge will be to illustrate this through our fallen human relationships. Assign each group one of the following groups of people: a family, a military unit, or an athletic team. The goal is to explain who provides the words, who reveals them, and how those words are explained and taught to the rest of the group. To get them started, you might have them start with structures. For example, an athletic team would have a coach, a captain, and team members—maybe even a mascot. How would these distinct expressions of one team be like or unlike the triune God?

Give several minutes for your teens to work out their illustrations. Then have each group act it out for the others.

QUESTIONS TO ASK

1. **What were some positive ways the Trinity was revealed through these presentations? What were some negative ways?**
2. **God has given the church the responsibility for being his representation on earth. How well do you think some of our relationships reveal the heart of God to those who don't know him? What are some ways we could improve?**

TRANSITIONAL TRUTH

Say something like—

> **When he was being tempted by Satan, Jesus said, "It is written: 'Man shall not live on bread alone, but on every word that comes from the mouth of God'" (Matthew 4:4). In other words, God's Word is as essential to our lives as food. We desperately and daily need to feed on God's Word. And God didn't only speak in times past; he continues to speak to us now. The question is, *Are we listening?***

MAKING IT PERSONAL
(10-15 MINUTES)

Start with something like—

> Sometimes it feels like work to read the Bible, right? It seems the same as reading any other book, and it's more about what we're doing than what God is doing. God has chosen to reveal himself in multiple ways, but we can know about them because he has spoken and continues to speak in and through the Bible. If God is speaking, then maybe our *reading* should be more about *listening* to his voice. Let's take a look at the Bible from this perspective.

OPTION 1:
FINE TUNING: A LISTENING ACTIVITY

Pass out the **Fine Tuning worksheets** for every individual in your group. Tell them how much time they will have for this activity, but encourage everyone not to rush. It might help if your teens spread out and find good listening spots away from any distractions. The idea is to slow down and listen as opposed to speed-reading. You can give everyone a heads-up when the time is nearly up. After you bring the group back together, ask them to share some of their thoughts. Also encourage your teens that they could do an activity like this every day if they would only commit 10 to 15 minutes.[5]

OPTION 2: ARE YOU LISTENING?

Play the video *Are You Listening?* When it's finished, ask the group the following questions.

[5]. To encourage your teens to go further with this concept, you may want to make copies available of the book *Enjoy the Silence* by Duffy and Maggie Robbins (Youth Specialties, 2005). You could even encourage your group to do this 30-day listening experiment together!

[6]. *Are You Listening*, directed by Church Fuel. Worship House Media, www.worshiphousemedia.com/mini-movies/20456/Are-You-Listening.

QUESTIONS TO ASK

1. When you read the Bible, do you hear more of your voice or God's? Explain.
2. How does this video portray the way we can or should hear from God?
3. What are some things you are doing or could do to be more in tune with God's voice and truly listening to his Word?

BRINGING IT TOGETHER

Finish with something like—

> God has spoken. He has and continues to speak in various ways. The Father gives the Word, the Son gives and lives it out, and the Spirit guides us into a deeper understanding of the Word. The question each of us has to continually ask ourselves is, *Am I listening?* Let's take a minute to pray for ourselves and each other as we learn to listen to God.

Pray—

> Our God who speaks, thank you for revealing yourself to us. We know you wouldn't have spoken if you had not wanted us to listen. May we ever be tuning in to your voice and obeying the word we hear. Father, we ask this through your Son and in the power of the Spirit—one God, forever and ever. Amen.

SESSION 2:
WITH A WORD

WORD FOR WORD
SMALL-GROUP WORKSHEET

1. Read Genesis 1:1-5 and compare it to Psalm 33:6-9. How did God choose to create?

2. Compare what you've just read with John 1:1-18. List your observations about "the Word" in this passage.

3. Read John 16:5-15. Who was to come when Jesus left? What would this person be doing?

4. Read John 14:23-26. Who seems to be the source of the words in this passage? Who speaks and lives out the words? Who guides and reminds us of the words? Do they speak whatever they want, or do they all say the same thing? Explain.

SESSION 2:
WITH A WORD

WORD FOR WORD
LEADER'S WORKSHEET

1. Read Genesis 1:1-5 and compare it to Psalm 33:6-9. How did God choose to create?
   These passages indicate that God spoke the world into existence with his very breath or with a word.

2. Compare what you've just read with John 1:1-18. List your observations about "the Word" in this passage.
   Personal observations will vary, but a few observations might be as follows:
   - *The Word was in the beginning.*
   - *The Word was with God (distinct).*
   - *The Word was God (the same).*
   - *The Word made all things.*
   - *The Word became flesh.*
   - *The Word is the one and only.*
   - *The Word has made God known to us.*

3. Read John 16:5-15. Who was to come when Jesus left? What would this person be doing?
   Jesus promises the Advocate or the Holy Spirit will come in Jesus' place. Some Bible translations call him the Counselor. A few of the activities observed would be as follows:
   - *Convict the world of sin*
   - *Guide Jesus' followers into all truth*
   - *Bring glory to Jesus*
   - *Make Jesus' life and words known to us*

4. Read John 14:23-26. Who seems to be the source of the words in this passage? Who speaks and lives out the words? Who guides and reminds us of the words? Do they speak whatever they want, or do they all say the same thing? Explain.
   The source is God the Father. The one who speaks and lives out before us is God the Son. God the Spirit teaches, reminds, and guides us into all truth. They are distinct in their expressions, but they all speak the same Word. In this we can see they are truly three and one.

SESSION 2:
WITH A WORD

FINE TUNING: A LISTENING ACTIVITY
SMALL-GROUP WORKSHEET

READING: PSALM 19

Open your Bible to the passage. Say a brief prayer: Ask God to give you a deeper understanding of his Word, and ask the Spirit to help you tune into God's voice. Then read the verses slowly. Take note of any words or phrases that stand out to you. You may want to mark your Bible or jot the words or phrases in the space below.

MEDITATION

Think about how this Bible passage describes the ways God speaks.

1. Read verses 1-6 again. How does God speak? Have you been listening?
2. Read verses 7-11 again. How does God speak? Have you been listening?
3. Read verses 12-14 again. How does God speak? (Think about how God works within you and where things are "hidden" and where we "meditate.") Have you been listening?

PRAYER

You may not be where you want to be, and that's okay. God wants you to come to him with an open heart and a mind willing to change. Take some time to talk to God about where you are spiritually and where you'd like to be. Consider using some of the wording from the Bible passage that stood out to you as you share your heart with God.

CONTEMPLATION

Take some moments of silence and imagination. Picture parts of God's creation that bring you joy and think about what God might be saying if you are listening. Imagine how your time reading the Bible would change if you focused on listening instead of just reading. Try to wrap your mind around the closeness you would feel with God if you really understood how well he knows you and how much he desires to have a relationship with you. Rest in these thoughts by concentrating on them for a few minutes.

Use the following space to write some key thoughts you want to remember and possibly share when your group gets back together.

OVERVIEW

In this session teens will consider the mission of God the Father, understand how that relates to the Son and Spirit, and begin to see how his plan affects their personal lives.

SETTING THE TONE

A relationship with God means more than a cozy spot in heaven. Our passionate, triune God is on a mission. This has been true of God from the very beginning, and making that mission is the special role and right of the Father. "From initial creation through ultimate consummation and everything that happens in between, it is God the Father who is the Architect, the Designer, the one who stands behind all that occurs as the one who plans and implements what he has chosen to do."[7]

7. Bruce Ware. *Father, Son, and Holy Spirit: Relationships, Roles, and Relevance* (Wheaton, Ill.: Crossway Books, 2005), 51.

Missio Dei is the Latin phrase meaning "the sending of God." The Father has sent his Son on his mission. The Father and Son have sent the Spirit on his mission. As theologian Andreas Köstenberger has said, "...the three persons of the Godhead are involved in one great mission, the revelation of God to humanity and the redemption of humanity for God."[8] God has revealed himself, and he chooses to use those who are in relationship with him to reach those who are not. This is an opportunity for us not only to see God's mission but to commit to being participants in that mission.

BREAKING THE ICE
(8-10 MINUTES)

OPTION 1: BROKEN

Say something like—

> We're going back to the beginning of time tonight. This great God we've been talking about created the world and saw that it was good. But something happened that took what God made good and broke it.

Play the video *Free Fall*. When the video is finished, ask your group the following questions.

QUESTIONS TO ASK

1. What struck you most while watching this clip?
2. Do you think the man and woman's choice to sin had any effect on God? If not, why? If so, how?
3. This video seems to end without any resolution of man's brokenness. Did God leave us that way? What does the Bible tells us?

8. Andreas Köstenberger and Scott Swain. *Father, Son and Spirit: The Trinity in John's Gospel* (Downers Grove, Ill.: IVP Academic, 2008), 155.

9. *Free Fall*, directed by Prolifik Films. Worship House Media, www.worshiphousemedia.com/mini-movies/18730/Free-Fall.

OPTION 2: THE FALL

Say something like—

> We're going back to the beginning of time
> tonight. This great God we've been talking
> about created the world and saw that it was
> good. But something happened that took
> what God made good and broke it.

Have a volunteer read or narrate Genesis 3. You may also
want to ask a few other volunteers to read those parts spoken
by the Serpent, Adam, and Eve. When the reading is finished,
ask the group the following questions.

QUESTIONS TO ASK

1. **What struck you most while listening to this
   story?**
2. **Do you think the man and woman's choice to sin
   had any effect on God? If not, why? If so, how?**
3. **This story seems to end without any resolution
   of man's brokenness. Did God leave us that way?
   What does the Bible tells us?**

TRANSITIONAL TRUTH

Say—

> In the middle of this chapter is the state-
> ment by God to the Serpent that "I will put
> enmity between you and the woman, and
> between your offspring and hers; he will
> crush your head, and you will strike his
> heel" (Genesis 3:15). So from the moment
> we were broken, God had a plan—a
> mission—that included a child who would
> defeat the Serpent and heal our brokenness.
> God is on a mission to save humanity from

eternal separation from himself because of sin. Let's take a closer look at God's mission and how the three persons of the Godhead go on mission together.

HEARING THE WORD
(12-15 MINUTES)

GOD ON A MISSION

Have the teens get into small groups; you can determine the number to fit your needs. Give each one a copy of the **God on a Mission worksheet**. The questions will take more time than usual, so plan to assign one question to each group or pair. Give your teens time to answer the questions. When most have finished, have each group share their answers with the rest of the class.

TRANSITIONAL TRUTH

Say something like—

> God has been moving from the split-second of humanity's fall. He has been and continues to be on a mission to bring us back into a relationship with him. He loves us so much that he was willing to send his Son to die himself in our place. Yet God still allows the choice to be ours. It would be interesting to think through how our responses to his loving mission might affect God.

YOU'LL NEED

- Copies of the **God on a Mission worksheet**
- Bibles
- Pens or pencils

SHARING YOUR PERSPECTIVE
(10-12 MINUTES)

A VIEW FROM THE OTHER SIDE

Create three teams to complete this role-playing exercise. Pass out one of the scenarios for each group, and ask them to act out the scenes. After each team concludes, ask the whole group the following questions.

QUESTIONS TO ASK

1. **What were some of the thoughts or emotions shown by the individual who was rescued or restored?**
2. **What were some thoughts or emotions shown by the individual who went on a mission to rescue or restore?**

YOU'LL NEED

• A copy of the **A View from the Other Side worksheet** cut into strips

TRANSITIONAL TRUTH

Say something like—

> God doesn't simply save us *from* eternal separation. God's desire is to save us *to* eternal relationship—community with God and community with other believers. Too many times we think that because we respond to God individually, then the benefits from God are only individual. But taking a quick look at how God will complete his mission gives us a different picture.

MAKING IT PERSONAL
(15-20 MINUTES)

YOU'LL NEED

- Drawing paper
- Paints or colored pencils
- Mellow or worshipful music and a way to play it

WHAT GOD'S MISSION LOOKS LIKE

Pass out enough paper, paints, or colored pencils for each teen. Tell them something along these lines—

> **We need to understand what God sees as the end of his mission. To give us a better picture of that, I'm going to read Revelation 21:1-7. As I read, start sketching what you think the end looks like for those who respond to the Spirit's conviction, believe in the Son, and receive the love of the Father. I'll read through the passage more than once, and you can keep sketching. After the reading, I'll put on some music for a few minutes to give you time to work. I'll call you back together when it's time to wrap up.**

Slowly read through the passage twice. Take time during the music to encourage each of your teens as they express their view of the end of God's mission. When you feel the time is right, bring everyone together for a time of sharing. Be sure to point out that God uses terms including *bride, husband, his people, inherit, their God,* and *my children.* All of these are terms of family and community. God hasn't saved us simply for our betterment but for a relationship with God and his people.

You can also ask your teens if they would be willing to let you display some of their work. Their art can be a reminder during the weeks ahead of the end of God's mission—our living in eternal community with him.

BRINGING IT TOGETHER

Finish with something like—

> God has been and still is on a mission. He doesn't want anyone to be separated from him because of sin. He wants all people to be restored to a relationship with him through the Son and in the power of the Spirit. We'll take the next few sessions to look more deeply into each aspect of God's mission. For now, let's be filled with awe that Almighty God would be in constant pursuit and on a mission to have a relationship with us.

Pray this or something similar—

> Our God, thank you for pursuing us even while we cared nothing about you. Thank you for not only saving us from eternal death—but for saving us to eternal life in community with you and with all those who call on your marvelous name. May we commit to live in ever deepening relationship with you and with each other. Father, we ask this through your Son and in the power of your Spirit—one God, forever and ever. Amen.

SESSION 3:
MISSIO DEI

GOD ON A MISSION
SMALL-GROUP WORKSHEET

1. Read Genesis 22:1-19. What did God ask Abraham to do? How did God provide an offering? How did God say all nations on earth would be blessed?

2. Read Isaiah 9:1-7. Isaiah provides hope to Abraham's descendants (Israel) in this passage. What are some of the things that stand out about this hopeful experience (word pictures, personal figures, etc.)? How does this compare to John 1:1-18 (from our last session)?

3. Read John 3:1-21. Who has God sent to see to it that men and women are able to be restored and be part of his kingdom? What are the key terms or descriptions of his mission?

4. Read John 15:26-16:15. Who has God sent to guide us to his truth? What are the key terms or descriptions of his mission?

SESSION 3: MISSIO DEI

GOD ON A MISSION
LEADER'S WORKSHEET

1. Read Genesis 22:1-19. What did God ask Abraham to do? How did God provide an offering? How did God say all nations on earth would be blessed?
   Here God asks Abraham to sacrifice his only son to God. (Isaac was the only son of Sarah and Abraham, and God had already allowed for Ishmael to be sent away. So Isaac was the only son for Abraham's line to continue.) When God saw Abraham's faith, he provided a substitute for Isaac in the form of a ram (v. 13). All nations would be blessed through Abraham's offspring or lineage (v. 18). Key: God's promise.

2. Read Isaiah 9:1-7. Isaiah provides hope to Abraham's descendants (Israel) in this passage. What are some of the things that stand out about this hopeful experience (word pictures, personal figures, etc.)? How does this compare to John 1:1-18 (from our last session)?
   Some things that may stand out include, but aren't limited to, people walking in darkness, seeing a great light, rejoicing, being set free, a male child is given who will reign, and the "zeal of the LORD Almighty will accomplish this." Compared to John 1, we see the contrast between dark and light as well as a male son who has made God known to the world. There is also an interesting note about being born of God as opposed to Abraham, though the unifying factor is faith or receiving God. Key: God's promise through his Son.

3. Read John 3:1-21. Who has God sent to see to it that men and women are able to be restored and be part of his kingdom? What are the key terms or descriptions of his mission?
   God has sent his one and only Son. Consider how this relates to the beginning promise with Abraham. Some key terms or descriptions may include—
   - *Believing in the Son is the way to be "born again" by the Spirit in order to become restored to a relationship with God.*
   - *Men love darkness rather than light.*
   - *The Son of Man will be lifted up for men and women to know and believe in him.*
   - *Key: God's promise through his Son to bring us back to a relationship with him.*

4. **Read John 15:26-16:15. Who has God sent to guide us to his truth? What are the key terms or descriptions of his mission?**

The Advocate, or Spirit, is sent by God the Father. The Spirit is also sent by God the Son. This shows the distinct positions and activities within the Trinity but does not negate that each is God. Some key terms or descriptions might include—

- *God the Spirit will prove the world to be in the wrong about sin, righteousness, and judgment.*
- *He will guide us into all truth.*
- *He will speak only what he hears.*
- *The Spirit will take what belongs to the Son and make it known to us.*
- *Key: God's promise through his Son to bring us back to a relationship with him through the work of the Spirit.*

SESSION 3:
MISSIO DEI

A VIEW FROM THE OTHER SIDE
ROLE-PLAY WORKSHEET

Make a copy of this sheet and cut out each scenario, or rewrite each one on a separate note card to pass out to your teams. Take each scenario in order to allow for the understanding to build. The final will be the clearest illustration of God on a mission for us.

SCENARIO 1

(2 people)

One person is waiting at a crosswalk of a busy street. She sees another person walking toward her from the other side, not paying any attention to the signals or oncoming traffic. When the first person sees this, she leaps into action and pushes the other out of the street and away from oncoming traffic. The rescued one stands, says, "What's your problem?" and continues to walk into traffic.

SCENARIO 2

(4 or more people)

A military special ops team is in the middle of a rescue mission. The team leader shares the plan and explains that this is what the hours of planning and training have prepared them to do. They move in and find their captured brother. They tell him it's time to go home, but the captive looks at the team leader, expresses thanks for planning and executing the mission, and says he's quite content to stay in his dark cell.

SCENARIO 3

(4 or more people)

A child has run away from home. The parents constantly look for her. Their friends discourage them from continuing their search, but they persevere. Finally they find their daughter. They explain how excited they are. She answers with reasons why she isn't worth their efforts. The father looks at her and says, "There is never a time when we don't love you, and there's nothing you can ever do to change that." The daughter responds by going with her parents, and the parents assure her that her siblings will be thrilled to have her back home.

MORNING SICKNESS
SESSION FOUR

OVERVIEW

This lesson investigates the virgin birth. Teens will consider the setting of Jesus' birth, understand what the virgin birth tells us about Jesus, and determine what this event means to their personal faith.

SETTING THE TONE

Over the years I've volunteered at crisis pregnancy centers in two different states. I haven't been on the front lines talking directly to the girls who come in, but I've done everything I can to help teens become aware of the consequences that come from sex before and outside of a marriage relationship. I've heard stories of girls at the pregnancy centers or from personal friends who have experienced deep regret and pain because of a bad sexual choice.

Imagine feeling that kind of uncertainty and stigma when you didn't do anything wrong! It's hard to know exactly what Mary felt and went through when her family and friends learned of her miracle pregnancy. But she was a young woman of great faith who became hopeful at the realization of who the baby growing inside her actually was.

There are some areas of our faith that are not optional, but completely essential. The virgin birth is one of those areas. This wasn't a special birth simply because it was some kind of medical marvel or a wonderful story—it was most important because it tells us about the Christ child. Jesus wasn't just anybody. He was God in the flesh. And because of this birth, our world was forever changed.

BREAKING THE ICE
(10-15 MINUTES)

YOU'LL NEED

• A copy of the movie *The Nativity Story*[10] and a way to play it

OPTION 1: THE NATIVITY STORY

PART 1

Begin your session with scene 7, "A Child through the Holy Spirit," from **The Nativity Story**. Stop the film after Mary says, "How are they to understand?" and ask the following questions.

QUESTIONS TO ASK

1. How did Mary respond to the news of her pregnancy?
2. What was Mary thinking as the others were sleeping?

PART 2

Continue by playing scene 11, "Mary Returns Home," from the movie. Stop after Mary says, "There is a will for this child greater than my fear of what they may do."

10. *The Nativity Story,* directed by Catherine Hardwicke (2006, New Line Cinema: 2007, New Line Home Entertainment, DVD).

QUESTIONS TO ASK

1. **What would you be thinking and feeling if you were Mary (or Joseph)?**
2. **Why do you think Jesus was born under these circumstances?**

OPTION 2: MARY'S PERSPECTIVE

Read the possible thoughts of Mary from pages 12-16 of Steven James' book *Never the Same*. As you read or when you've finished, ask the following questions.

QUESTIONS TO ASK

1. **What would you be thinking and feeling if you were Mary (or Joseph)?**
2. **Why do you think Jesus was born under these circumstances?**

TRANSITIONAL TRUTH

Say something like—

> As we've discussed before, Scripture prophesied about the coming of Jesus, the Messiah, as early as Genesis 3:15: "And I will put enmity between you and the woman, and between your offspring and hers; he will crush your head, and you will strike his heel." Matthew records in his account, "All this took place to fulfill what the Lord had said through the prophet: 'The virgin will conceive and give birth to a son, and they will call him Immanuel' (which means 'God with us')" (Matthew 1:22-23). But what does the virgin birth have to do with Jesus being God?

11. Steven James, *Never the Same* (El Cajon, Calif.: Youth Specialties, 2005). Let me encourage you to grab a copy of this book if you haven't already. It has provided a *This is real!* moment for me and my teens as we've used it in a small group. Using the first chapter of this book might kick off a small group or book discussion with teens at another time during the week.

HEARING THE WORD
(10-15 MINUTES)

GETTING THE STORIES STRAIGHT

Have your teens get into small groups; you can determine the number to fit the size of your class. Hand each one a copy of the **Getting the Stories Straight worksheet**. You may want to assign one or two questions to each group so they can be more thorough in their answers. When most have finished, have each group share their answers with the large group.

TRANSITIONAL TRUTH

Continue with something like—

> Apologist Alex McFarland says, "The virgin birth is central to establishing that Jesus is God."[12] If Jesus isn't God, then our faith is empty. If Jesus had been conceived from Joseph's seed, then Jesus would have been just a man—a great man, but only a man. 1 Corinthians 15:21-22 tells us, "For since death came through a man, the resurrection of the dead comes also through a man. For as in Adam all die, so in Christ all will be made alive." If Jesus had been born any other way than by the Holy Spirit, our faith would be hopeless. The question is—why?

12. Alex McFarland, *Stand: Core Truths You Must Know for an Unshakable Faith* (Carol Stream, Ill.: Tyndale House, 2005), 37.

SHARING YOUR PERSPECTIVE
(8-10 MINUTES)

TASTING A DIFFERENCE

Before you begin this session, get two mugs of water, two regular tea bags, and two clear plastic cups. Pour a tablespoon of salt into one plastic cup and a tablespoon of sugar into the other. During the session, tell your group—

> **To everyone in town Mary looked the same as any other pregnant girl. Many may have even assumed Joseph was the father. Nothing was different on the outside, but things were not as they appeared.**

Choose two volunteers to drink some hot tea. Have the clear cups in front of them along with the tea bags. Let them each prepare and heat their tea in the microwave. After a taste test, discuss the following questions.

QUESTIONS TO ASK

1. **Everything looked the same on the outside, but did the drinks taste the same? If not, what was different?**
2. **Assuming Jesus is the sweet tea and Joseph's (and Adam's) line is the salty, how would you describe Mary's pregnancy?**

TRANSITIONAL TRUTH

Continue with—

> **You see, God provided a very "sweet" gift in the miraculous conception of Jesus. Jesus was**

God. God came to us, though, as a man—in a way we could relate. He did this on purpose in order to save us, just as his birth name says. Jesus alludes to this in a parable found in Matthew 18:12-14, "What do you think? If a man owns a hundred sheep, and one of them wanders away, will he not leave the ninety-nine on the hills and go to look for the one that wandered off? And if he finds it, truly I tell you, he is happier about that one sheep than about the ninety-nine that did not wander off. In the same way your Father in heaven is not willing that any of these little ones should perish."

God doesn't want you to be alone. He wants to be with you, to be your God, to be your hope. If this is true, then what does that mean for you?

MAKING IT PERSONAL
(12-15 MINUTES)

Say—

Let's take some time to think about what Jesus' miraculous beginning means to each of us personally. During this time you can choose whichever option you'd like to express your thoughts.

Explain the two options below to your teens.

OPTION 1: A BEAUTIFUL PICTURE

Have paper and markers handy for those who would like to draw a scene or series of scenes to express what this truth

YOU'LL NEED

- Paper
- Markers or pencils

means to them. They might recreate the parable you've just shared and insert themselves into the scene or create something else entirely.

OPTION 2: A PERSONAL PARABLE

Have paper and pencils ready for teens to write out a story like the one Jesus told. They could rewrite the parable with their names inserted or create a more personalized story of where they are in their relationship with Jesus. When everyone is done, have your teens share their stories and pictures with each another.

BRINGING IT TOGETHER

Finish with—

> How Jesus came to earth is essential to our faith. It's necessary for Jesus to be God so we can have that perfect example and sacrifice which we'll study later. Jesus as a human is important because we need someone to touch, feel, see, and experience. God knew that. We'll take a closer look at his humanity next time. For now, let's thank God for Jesus' humble yet miraculous birth.

Pray—

> God, we thank you for the gift of the Son through the miracle of the virgin birth. It shows us your desire to be with us and to relate to us in a real and personal way. Please keep us passionate in our desire to be in relationship with you. Father, we ask this through your Son and in the power of the Spirit—one God, forever and ever. Amen.

SESSION 4:
MORNING SICKNESS

GETTING THE STORIES STRAIGHT
SMALL-GROUP WORKSHEET

1. Take another look at the announcement of Jesus' birth to Mary in Luke 1:28-35. List some things that stand out to you about what the angel said and how Mary responded.

2. Take a look at the announcement of the angel to Joseph in Matthew 1:18-25. List some things that stand out to you about what the angel said and how Joseph responded.

3. Now compare and contrast the two accounts. What things are common between the two stories?

4. Read John 14:7-11. What do you think Jesus was trying to tell his disciples?

5. Why do you think it's so important for Jesus to be God?

SESSION 4: MORNING SICKNESS

GETTING THE STORIES STRAIGHT
LEADER'S WORKSHEET

1. Take another look at the announcement of Jesus' birth to Mary in Luke 1:28-35. List some things that stand out to you about what the angel said and how Mary responded.
   Mary was afraid of this angel's arrival, so God's support and favor would no doubt have been comforting considering the message. Mary would give birth to a son and name him Jesus, and he would be called the Son of the Most High. He would be a king in the line of David, but he would reign forever. Mary didn't know how this could happen because she had never had sex. The angel said the Holy Spirit would come and bring about conception of this child.

2. Take a look at the announcement of the angel to Joseph in Matthew 1:18-25. List some things that stand out to you about what the angel said and how Joseph responded.
   Joseph found out that he was engaged to a pregnant woman, and he knew he hadn't been involved! He was a godly person, and his love for Mary is shown in that he feared both his involvement and Mary being harmed. The angel said to not fear because the whole thing was done by the Holy Spirit. Joseph was to name the baby Jesus. Joseph awoke from his dream and did exactly what the angel said, and he avoided any possible confusion about this being his child by not having sex with Mary until the child was born.

3. Now compare and contrast the two accounts. What things are common between the two stories?
   Mary and Joseph should not fear, but trust in God's plan. They were both told that this child was born of the Holy Spirit and not of any man—he was the Son of God. They both did as the angel instructed.

4. Read John 14:7-11. What do you think Jesus was trying to tell his disciples?
   Jesus said that he and the Father were in each other. In other words, they were one and the same. Jesus was God in the flesh.

5. Why do you think it's so important for Jesus to be God?
   This is open to a variety of answers that should give you some greater insight into your teens' understanding of who Jesus is and what he really means to the world and to them personally.

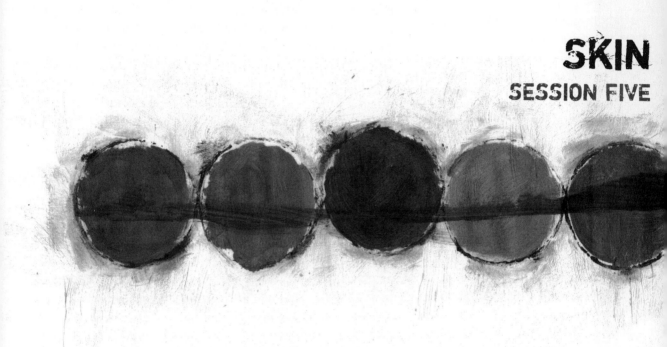

OVERVIEW

The purpose of this lesson is to focus on Jesus as a both fully God and fully human. Teens will discover the many indications of Jesus' humanity and deity, understand how he can fully relate to us, and begin to see and experience God on a personal level.

SETTING THE TONE

Have you ever visited an art gallery? If so, you'll understand what I'm about to say. You can pass by hundreds of works of art—some are nice and others might be kind of weird. But eventually one will totally seem to be speaking to you. You can stop and stare at it forever and still not feel like you've fully processed it.

The incarnation—Jesus becoming human—is like that. It demands our attention and careful consideration. We can gaze at Jesus for what seems like eternity, but all the words in the world don't seem enough to describe who he is and what he means to us. They say a picture's worth a thousand words. And in Jesus, the Word is painted. Instead of simply talking through it, let's try to paint a biblical picture of Jesus and allow the Spirit to guide us into all truth.

When we study the Trinity, we walk a fine line between our *ideas* about God and the *reality* of who he is. The incarnation puts flesh on all of our ideas, and we need to be sure we present a clear view of Jesus as God and man without missing the fact that Jesus came to bring us into community with God. Jesus' life and ministry give us a picture of life in God's kingdom, and he welcomes us to become citizens of that kingdom. To put it another way—in Jesus we see what life is like at the Father's house, and our trust in Jesus gives us the Spirit of adoption into God's family. May this session be a gallery of images that will capture the attention of your teens and exhort them to contemplate what the incarnation means to them.

BREAKING THE ICE
(8-10 MINUTES)

OPTION 1: A DEEPER UNDERSTANDING

Begin your session by showing part of *Batman Begins*. Play the end of scene 8, "Carmine Falcone," and the beginning of scene 9, "Embrace Your Fear" (approximately 28:25-32:07 on the DVD counter). When you stop the film, discuss the following questions.

[13.] *Batman Begins,* directed by Christopher Nolan (2005, Warner Bros. Pictures: 2006, Warner Home Video, DVD).

QUESTIONS TO ASK

1. What caused Bruce Wayne to give up everything?
2. How would you describe the ease or difficulty of his life after he made the decision to walk away?
3. How is Bruce's mission to understand similar to God's mission in Jesus to relate to us? How is it different?

OPTION 2: LIFE IN MY SHOES

Have your teens get in groups of two or three to act out one of the scenes from the worksheet found at the end of this session. Say—

> Luke 2:52 says, "And Jesus grew in wisdom and stature, and in favor with God and man." So Jesus went through teenage life, too. We're going to take a few minutes to picture what it might have looked like if Jesus had lived through a recent situation from your life. Choose one scene in your groups, and plan to act it out for the rest of us. Be sure to let us know who is playing Jesus so we can see how you think he might have responded in the situation.

After all the groups have acted out their scenes, ask these questions.

QUESTIONS TO ASK

1. Do the Jesus responses in our skits line up with what we know about God? Why or why not?
2. How easy or hard do you think it was for Jesus to grow up?
3. What does thinking about Jesus in this way tell you about how much God desires to be in a relationship with us?

TRANSITIONAL TRUTH

Say—

> The Father's master plan involved sending his Son to be born to a virgin and to live life as a human. Theologians call this the incarnation, which means that God took on human form. Jesus is God and man— one person with two natures.[14] As God, his power was limitless, but he accepted the limitation of being human. He did all this to show us what the Father is like (John 14:6-13) and to make a way to restore us to a relationship with God. We're going to look at a few scenes from Jesus' life to gain a better idea of who Jesus is and what the incarnation means to us.

HEARING THE WORD
(8-10 MINUTES)

SCENES FROM THE LIFE OF JESUS

Have the teens get into small groups; you can determine the number to fit your needs. Give each one a copy of the **Scenes from the Life of Jesus worksheet** found at the end of this session. Assign each group one scene to read and discuss. When most have finished, have each group share their answers with the large group. If you just used Option 2, then you'll use this time to discuss each scene more deeply. You might choose to transition directly from acting to discussing.

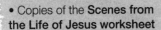

YOU'LL NEED

- Copies of the **Scenes from the Life of Jesus worksheet**
- Bibles
- Pens or pencils

[14.] This is an incredibly important doctrine called the *hypostatic union* that cannot be fully explained here, but the hope is for teens to uncover this truth throughout the session. See Fred Sanders and Klaus Issler, *Jesus in Trinitarian Perspective: An Introductory Christology* (Nashville, Tenn.: B&H Publishing, 2007) for a more detailed explanation of this doctrine that was hammered out in AD 451 at the Chalcedon Council.

TRANSITIONAL TRUTH

Say—

> We can talk about God's desire to relate to us, but words just don't seem to be enough to express why the incarnation is so important. The scenes we've just discussed are packed full of details that can easily be lost in all of our talk. For now let's focus on snapshots from each of these scenes and see if we can visualize these ideas about God as reality.

SHARING YOUR PERSPECTIVE
(15-20 MINUTES)

SNAPSHOTS OF TRUTH

Say something like—

> Think about the Bible verses you read in your groups. Create an artistic piece to express whatever part stands out to you. Be as creative as you can. The idea is to express some part of the incarnation and what it means to you. You'll have a chance to share your insights and inspirations for your artwork when we're finished.

Make the art materials available, and play some music in the background while the teens work. When the time is up, bring everyone together and encourage your teens to share their perspectives on the incarnation with the rest of the group. If some haven't made it far with their creations by the time limit, encourage them to share their concept and to finish their piece later for the gallery you'll have in the room.

YOU'LL NEED

- Art supplies (butcher paper, markers, easels, paints, whatever you have)
- Worshipful music and a way to play it

TRANSITIONAL TRUTH

Say—

> To this point, we've seen how God has gone to great lengths to relate to us in a real and personal way. But there's a danger in thinking there is only a one-to-one relationship between you and God. Remember, God hasn't simply saved us from eternal separation from him, but he has saved us to an eternal life in his family. In fact, all who believe in Christ are referred to as the body. Paul explains, "The body is a unit, though it is made up of many parts; and though all its parts are many, they form one body. So it is with Christ" (1 Corinthians 12:12, NIV1984). Did you hear that? We the church make up the body, and Paul compares that to Christ. If the incarnation reveals God with skin on, then the church is meant to put skin on the heart of God for the world.

MAKING IT PERSONAL
(10-15 MINUTES)

WHO DO YOU SAY JESUS IS?

Start with something like—

> In Matthew 16:13 Jesus asked his disciples, "Who do people say the Son of Man is?" People around us may know little or nothing about Jesus, or they might have some really outrageous ideas that don't match

the Bible at all. The Father left us as his representatives in the world to share and show what God is like. So it's important for each of us to think carefully about Jesus' next question in Matthew 16:15, "But what about you? Who do you say I am?"

Each of us has important decisions to make or difficult situations we're working through. Even in the midst of those we have the responsibility and benefit of sharing life with our brothers and sisters in Christ because God has saved us to his family. So for the next few minutes you'll have a chance to share a decision or struggle that is on your heart and mind. The rest of the group will share some encouragement based on what we know about who Jesus is and about the heart of our triune God. Then we'll say a sentence or two in prayer for each person.

If you have a large group, you'll probably want to assign a few group leaders who can lead the sharing and praying. The focus here is to build on the sense of community that we are to have in the Spirit and reinforce the idea that our study of the Trinity (especially as represented by the incarnation) reveals God's heart for relationship to himself and to each other.

BRINGING IT TOGETHER

Finish with something like—

God went to the most incredible lengths by humbly coming to relate to us in a tangible way. Nothing could be clearer about how much he wanted relationship with humans

than becoming a human. As we've said before, Jesus as God is necessary so we can have a perfect example and sacrifice for our sins (which we'll study later). And Jesus as a human is important because we need someone to touch, feel, see, and experience. God knew that.

We'll discover even more about Jesus' coming to earth in our future sessions. For now, let's praise God for taking on skin and showing us what he's really like.

Pray—

Father, you are almighty, yet you chose to come to us as a humble human. Thank you for the gift of knowing you through your Son, Jesus Christ. May we always keep our eyes on him and continue to know you more through the guidance of the Holy Spirit. We ask this through your Son and in the power of the Spirit—one God, forever and ever. Amen.

SESSION 5:
SKIN

SCENES FROM THE LIFE OF JESUS
SMALL-GROUP WORKSHEET

Read the Bible passage for your assigned scene and discuss your responses to the questions below.

SCENE 1: THE TEMPTATION (LUKE 4:1-14)

1. How do you see the Trinity in this passage (Father, Son, and Spirit)?

2. What does this show you about Jesus' deity?

3. What does this show you about Jesus' humanity?

4. How does Hebrews 4:14-16 relate?

SCENE 2: THE BAPTISM (JOHN 1:19-34)

1. How do you see the Trinity in this passage (Father, Son, and Spirit)?

2. What does this show you about Jesus' deity?

3. What does this show you about Jesus' humanity?

4. What differences or similarities do you see in Matthew 3:13-17?

SCENE 3: THE HEALING (LUKE 5:17-26)

1. How do you see the Trinity in this passage (Father, Son, and Spirit)?

2. What does this show you about Jesus' deity?

3. What does this show you about Jesus' humanity?

4. How does Acts 10:37-38 describe Jesus' ministry?

SESSION 5:
SKIN

SCENES FROM THE LIFE OF JESUS
LEADER'S WORKSHEET

Read the Bible passage for your assigned scene and discuss your responses to the questions below.

SCENE 1: THE TEMPTATION (LUKE 4:1-14)

1. How do you see the Trinity in this passage (Father, Son, and Spirit)?

   The Father is implied throughout in the phrase "Son of God" as well as pronoun references, such as, "He will command his angels concerning you to guard you carefully." The Father demonstrates authority. The Son is the focus of the passage, and we can see his humanity and alignment with the Father's will. The Spirit is on Jesus and even leads Jesus (v. 1) into the wilderness.

2. What does this show you about Jesus' deity?

   The devil questions Jesus' deity, but Jesus doesn't give a clear response to affirm his deity here. There are some implications of his deity, and responses may vary.

3. What does this show you about Jesus' humanity?

   Jesus' humanity is clearly seen in the fact that he was hungry (v. 2). Also, the fact that Jesus was tempted reveals his humanity because James 1:13 tells us God cannot be tempted. However, this fact does not mean that Jesus was not God. He is God and man—one person with two natures. His human nature is what's being tempted here in this passage.

4. How does Hebrews 4:14-16 relate?

   Jesus understands our temptations but serves as a perfect model of a life committed to the Father's will in the power of the Spirit. We can go to God with confidence that he knows and understands our every need.

SCENE 2: THE BAPTISM (JOHN 1:19-34)

1. How do you see the Trinity in this passage (Father, Son, and Spirit)?

   The Spirit came down on the Son as a dove, and the Father is the "one who sent me to baptize." This is further elaborated in Matthew 3 (below). The Father initiates the plan, the focus is the Son, and the Spirit directs our focus to the Son.

2. What does this show you about Jesus' deity?

John refers to Jesus as the "Lamb of God, who takes away the sin of the world!" Only God can forgive sins. John further testifies that Jesus is "God's Chosen One," or the "Son of God" as other Bible translations say.

3. What does this show you about Jesus' humanity?

Some sample responses could be that Jesus was seen as human—able to be seen, touched, baptized, etc.

4. What differences or similarities do you see in Matthew 3:13-17?

Jesus shows his commitment to the Father's plan ("proper for us to do this to fulfill all righteousness"). The voice from heaven says, "This is my Son," revealing the voice to be that of the Father.

SCENE 3: THE HEALING (LUKE 5:17-26)

1. How do you see the Trinity in this passage (Father, Son, and Spirit)?

The Father and the Spirit are not referred to specifically in this passage. The Son is the focus. But the purpose in continuing to ask this question is to get teens to be thinking in a Trinitarian way even if the Trinity is not expressly stated in a particular Bible passage. There could be a variety of implied thoughts of the Father and Spirit, but the focus here is on the Son.

2. What does this show you about Jesus' deity?

Jesus forgave the man's sins—something that could only be done by God himself. Jesus also knew what the men were thinking which may serve as an example of our all-knowing (omniscient) God. Jesus claims to have authority to forgive sins, but he also exhibits the ability to miraculously heal.

3. What does this show you about Jesus' humanity?

Answers may vary, but his humanity is expressed in his presence and interaction with the people.

4. How does Acts 10:37-38 describe Jesus' ministry?

Here we find help in answering our first question on the activity of the Father and Spirit in times like the healing of the paralytic. God the Father anointed Jesus with the Holy Spirit and power. As a result Jesus "went around doing good and healing all who were under the power of the devil, because God was with him."

A BEAUTIFUL DEATH
SESSION SIX

OVERVIEW

This session will take a reflective look at Jesus' death. Teens will consider the setting of the crucifixion, understand what Jesus' death means to them personally, and evaluate their lives in view of his sacrifice.

SETTING THE TONE

Sacrifice has become a relatively everyday word, but it held much deeper significance in the cultures represented in Scripture. Through-out the Bible we see sacrifices and offerings being made for sins, thanks, dedications, and more. Today we talk of little sacrifices we have to make to get through the day, to get ahead toward our life goals, and to make relationships work. We have a limited view of what true sacrifice is.

Our view will remain limited until we grasp what it is that the Father did through the Son at the cross. The cross is a terrible sight to behold, but the image ultimately gives us hope. The suffering experienced there was unspeakable, yet we proudly display the symbol of shame because of what it means. The important thing is that we truly know what it means.

Before this session, spend some extra time in prayer for your teens as you prepare to go together to the cross and reflect on what happened there. Keep in mind "the Spirit must awaken our hearts to see the beauty of Christ, fall before him, and put our hope and trust in him."[15] Pray also that your teens will be able to say that their hope and trust is in the one true God who loved them enough to die in their place.

BREAKING THE ICE
(15-20 MINUTES)

OPTION 1: THE CROSS—A MULTISENSORY EXPERIENCE

You might consider playing a worship song such as "The Wonderful Cross" at the beginnng of your session to help your teens focus their thoughts. Begin by saying—

> **We're taking time now to reflect on Jesus' death on the cross. Before we get started, let's all take a minute or two in silent prayer to ask the Father to open our hearts and minds through the power of the Spirit to see and understand Jesus' sacrifice for us on the cross. I'll let you know when the time is up.**

Have the teens break into small groups; you can decide how many. Be sure each group has a table of sensory elements

15. Ware, *Father, Son, and Holy Spirit*, 121.

ready and available to use for the reading. Use **The Cross—A Multisensory Experience** leader's guide at the end of this chapter as you do the reading. When you have finished, ask the teens the following questions.

QUESTIONS TO ASK

1. **What were some of your thoughts or feelings during this experience?**
2. **What person or people stood out to you?**
3. **Why did the Father send the Son to do this?**

OPTION 2: THE PASSION

Please use discretion if you choose to make use of this graphic video option. Begin by saying—

> **We're taking time now to reflect on Jesus' death on the cross. Before we get started, let's all take a minute or two in silent prayer to ask the Father to open our hearts and minds through the power of the Spirit to see and understand Jesus' sacrifice for us on the cross. I'll let you know when the time is up.**

Play *The Passion of the Christ*. Begin partway through scene 8, "The Eighth Station of the Cross: Jesus Meets the Woman of Jerusalem," as Jesus gets help carrying the cross through the streets, and end when Jesus looks up to heaven in scene 9, "The Ninth Station of the Cross: Jesus Falls the Third Time (approximately 1:27:27-1:34:08 on the DVD counter. After watching, ask your teens the following questions.

QUESTIONS TO ASK

1. **What were some of your thoughts or feelings during this experience?**
2. **What person or people stood out to you?**
3. **Why did the Father send the Son to do this?**

---

16. *The Passion of the Christ*, directed by Mel Gibson (2004, Icon Productions: 2004, 20th Century Fox, DVD).

TRANSITIONAL TRUTH

Say—

> Not only did the Father send his Son to die, but Jesus willingly gave up his life for ours. We're going to be "fixing our eyes on Jesus, the pioneer and perfecter of faith. For the joy set before him he endured the cross, scorning its shame, and sat down at the right hand of the throne of God" (Hebrews 12:2). Let's take a look at what this terrible yet beautiful death meant then and what it means to us now.

HEARING THE WORD
(8-10 MINUTES)

A WILLING SACRIFICE

Arrange your teens in small groups; you can determine the number to fit your needs. Hand each one a copy of the **A Willing Sacrifice worksheet**. Each group will work through all the Bible references and discuss them. When most have finished, have each group share some thoughts with the large group.

TRANSITIONAL TRUTH

Say something like—

> Our triune God made an incredible sacrifice that cut to the core of who he is in order to have a relationship with us. By making a commitment to follow Christ, we also make a

decision to place our lives in him. So if Jesus was misunderstood, then shouldn't we expect to be misunderstood too? Paul said in Philippians 1:29, "For it has been granted to you on behalf of Christ not only to believe on him, but also to suffer for him." Following Christ means being willing—just as he was—to suffer and sacrifice so God will be glorified.

SHARING YOUR PERSPECTIVE
(8-10 MINUTES)

TOUGH DECISIONS

Pass out a few index cards to each person. Say something like—

> We will all have to make some tough decisions as we follow Jesus. Some of you already have; others will sooner or later. Let's think about how we might respond to some situations that have or might come up.

Ask your teens to write a situation that either has happened or might happen that would challenge their commitment to follow Christ. You'll also want to prepare a few ideas of your own to add to the mix to encourage conversation. Some ideas might include—

- Risking rejection by resisting pressure from friends to sin
- Responding to name-calling and criticism for going to church or youth group
- Being ridiculed for standing up for people who can't stand up for themselves

YOU'LL NEED
- Index cards
- Pens or pencils

As the ideas seem to slow down, collect all of the cards and read each situation. Invite the group to give their ideas about how to respond and remind each other of the commitment Christ made for us.

TRANSITIONAL TRUTH

Say—

> **Second Corinthians 4:6 says, "For God, who said, 'Let light shine out of darkness,' made his light shine in our hearts to give us the light of the knowledge of God's glory displayed in the face of Christ." In Jesus' face we can see the joy, the pain, the intensity, the sorrow, and the determination that Jesus experienced as he paved the way for us to be restored to a relationship with God and in right relationships with each other.**

MAKING IT PERSONAL
(10-12 MINUTES)

WORKING IT OUT

You'll want to prepare ahead of time for this exercise. Sketch an outline of a person's head and shoulders on a piece of poster board or large paper to hang on a wall in your meeting room. The teens will be posting their ideas on your outline to fill out the image of the face of Christ.

Have the teens get into groups, and give each group a stack of sticky notes. Tell them—

> **The Father has sent his Son as an example of a willing sacrifice, and he calls us to fol-**

low in Jesus' steps. However, he hasn't left us to do this in our own power. God the Spirit works to begin developing the character of Christ in our lives.

Ask the groups to choose one person to read Philippians 2:1-13. As they listen, they should write out a word on each sticky note that describes a characteristic of Christ or a characteristic that should show in a believer's life. When they finish reading and writing, the teens should go and fill in the sketched outline with their notes.

When the groups have finished, ask the following questions.

QUESTIONS TO ASK

1. Which characteristics describe Jesus?
2. What is the only conditional—if—statement listed in this passage? Who should this passage also describe?
3. Does this image relate only to our personal relationship with God, or does it affect our relationships with others as well? Explain using examples.
4. As you "work out your salvation," where do you get the power to continue (v. 13)?
5. *(You might want your teens to reflect on this silently.)* How does your life compare to the face of Christ shown here? What are some areas that you need to submit to the Spirit's work?

BRINGING IT TOGETHER

Finish with something like—

The Father sent the Son to give himself up as a willing sacrifice who would pave the way to a relationship with God. As followers of Jesus, our lives should reflect that same attitude as we work out our salvation in the power of the Spirit. In light of what Jesus did for us, may each of us respond well to whatever God calls us to willingly sacrifice for him.

Pray something like this—

Father, thank you for pouring out your love for us through the death of your Son. Please help us each to see the areas we still haven't committed to you, and let the Spirit empower us to reflect the beautiful sacrifice made by Jesus. Father, we ask this through your Son and in the power of the Spirit—one God, forever and ever. Amen.

PREPARATION NOTE

As a heads-up, check out all the activity options for Session 8. You'll need to schedule your special guests ahead of time to help connect your teens to the larger family of God.

SESSION 6:
A BEAUTIFUL DEATH

THE CROSS—A MULTISENSORY EXPERIENCE
LEADER'S GUIDE

Read John 19 out loud to walk your group through the crucifixion. Below is a guide for reading and facilitating the multisensory experience. Note that you'll want to prepare the sensory elements ahead of time and lay them on tables for teens to use in small groups.

1. Have teens hold or pass around the thorny branches as you read verses 1-5.
2. Have teens hold or pass around the purple fabric as you read verses 6-16.
3. Have teens hold or pass around a large nail or railroad spike while you read verses 17-22. When you read verse 18, pause and pound the hammer three times on the board. When you read verse 19, pound the hammer once more and continue reading.
4. Have teens hold or pass around the white fabric as you read verses 23-24.
5. Have teens smell and taste the vinegar while you read verses 25-29.
6. Ask everyone to be silent and still while you read verse 30. Observe a moment of silence.
7. Have everyone remain still while you read verses 31-37.
8. Have teens smell the oil or spices as you read verses 38-42.

SESSION 6:
A BEAUTIFUL DEATH

A WILLING SACRIFICE
SMALL-GROUP WORKSHEET

1. Read Mark 14:32-42. What do you see here of Jesus' deity and humanity? Do you think Jesus' prayers reveal his unwillingness to die or his commitment to continue? Explain.

2. Read John 18:1-11. Does Jesus go willingly? What do you think he meant in verse 11?

3. Think about this statement regarding how the Romans would have seen Jesus: "Death on the cross was the penalty for slaves, as everyone knew; as such it symbolized extreme humiliation, shame and torture."[17] Now read Deuteronomy 21:23. How do you think the Jewish people would have looked at Jesus? Now read Galatians 3:13. Describe what Jesus did for us in your own words.

4. Think about Jesus' words in Matthew 27:46. What does this statement reveal to us about the Trinity? How did the crucifixion affect the relationship of the three in one?

5. The Father sent his Son to willingly sacrifice himself for us. Read John 3:16-18. Why did the Father do this according to these verses? (Please let a leader know if you would like to discuss this further either in the group or one-on-one.)

17. Martin Hengel, *Crucifixion in the Ancient World and the Folly of the Message of the Cross,* (Philadelphia, Pa.: Fortress Press, 1977), 62.

SESSION 6:
A BEAUTIFUL DEATH

A WILLING SACRIFICE
LEADER'S WORKSHEET

1. Read Mark 14:32-42. What do you see here of Jesus' deity and humanity? Do you think Jesus' prayers reveal his unwillingness to die or his commitment to continue? Explain.
   Jesus calls God his Father and willingly submits to the Father's will. We also see his soul overwhelmed with sorrow and his desire for support from his closest friends. Jesus asks for the cup of God's wrath to be removed, if possible (humanity), but he is committed to do the Father's will as opposed to his own.

2. Read John 18:1-11. Does Jesus go willingly? What do you think he meant in verse 11?
   Jesus does go willingly. His actions reveal that he didn't want a military revolt to fight for his cause. Instead he tells Peter to put his sword away. Jesus is resigned to accept—not fight—the cup of God's wrath on our behalf.

3. Think about this statement regarding how the Romans would have seen Jesus: "Death on the cross was the penalty for slaves, as everyone knew; as such it symbolized extreme humiliation, shame and torture."[18] Now read Deuteronomy 21:23. How do you think the Jewish people would have looked at Jesus? Now read Galatians 3:13. Describe what Jesus did for us in your own words.
   Jesus would have been viewed by the Romans and Jews as a common criminal with no honor before the people or God. It was absolutely shameful to be crucified. But Jesus wasn't the offender—we are. Galatians tells us that Jesus became the curse for us. Doing this allowed us to receive the blessing and promise given to Abraham (Genesis 22:15-18) and to receive by faith the promise of the Spirit. (We'll discuss the Spirit more in Session 8.)

4. Think about Jesus' words in Matthew 27:46. What does this statement reveal to us about the Trinity? How did the crucifixion affect the relationship of the three in one?
   Jesus is God, yet he is talking to God. We can clearly see the difference between the Son and the Father here. And we can also see what's happening in the perfect relationship of the Son with the Father. Jesus is crying out that the Father has forsaken or abandoned him. By taking on the sins of the world, God was willing to sacrifice the very core of who he is as a Trinity to make a way for our restored relationship with him.

[18.] Hengel, *Crucifixion*, 62.

5. The Father sent his Son to willingly sacrifice himself for us. Read John 3:16-18. Why did the Father do this according to these verses? (Please let a leader know if you would like to discuss this further either in the group or one-on-one.)

The Father sent his Son out of love so that we wouldn't have to die and be separated from him—instead we can be restored to him and have eternal life. We need to be saved from eternal separation because of sin (see also Romans 3:23). Believing in Jesus brings the gift of eternal life (Acts 16:31).

EMPTY
SESSION SEVEN

OVERVIEW

The purpose of this session is to reveal the hope of Jesus' resurrection. Teens will examine the resurrection, understand its importance to their faith, and find or renew hope in the life Jesus came to offer them.

SETTING THE TONE

God has been on a mission since the garden to restore humanity to a right relationship with himself. The death of God the Son wasn't the end of that mission. In fact, Jesus' death would have held no power at all without his resurrection. As Mark Driscoll and Gerry Breshears wrote in *Doctrine*, "Apart from the resurrection of Jesus Christ, there is no savior, no salvation, no forgiveness of sin, and no hope of resurrected eternal life."[19] The resurrection of Christ is the central event

19. Mark Driscoll and Gerry Breshears, *Doctrine: What Christians Should Believe* (Wheaton, Ill.: Crossway Books, 2010), 279.

in the history of the church. This has remained constant from the event itself to the present day. As believers today we agree with the first Christians who "were completely convinced that the resurrection did not merely demonstrate the existence of God, but represented God's endorsement of Jesus' mission."[20]

By definition resurrection does not mean simply coming back to life. That would be true of anyone who was *revived*, yet would simply die another day, such as Lazarus. To experience resurrection is to come back to life and live forever. And the doctrine of the resurrection is what brings us true hope and peace that we will be raised to an eternity in perfect relationship with God and one another. As Christians we cannot overlook this crucial event. We need to relay the centrality of the resurrection to teens as they grow in the faith and understanding of our triune God. Driscoll and Breshears said it well: "In closing, no one can remain neutral regarding Jesus' resurrection. The claim is too staggering, the event is too earthshaking, the implications are too significant, and the matter is too serious. We must each either receive or reject it as truth for us, and to remain indifferent or undecided is to reject it."[21]

BREAKING THE ICE
(8-10 MINUTES)

OPTION 1: VOICES OF THE CROSS

Gather everyone together and begin by playing the video *Voices of the Cross*. When the video is finished, move to the following questions.

QUESTIONS TO ASK

1. Describe some of the thoughts and emotions of those voices of the cross.

20. McGrath, *Understanding the Trinity*, 38-39.

21. Driscoll and Breshears. *Doctrine*, 303.

22. *Voices of the Cross*, directed by Dan Stevers. Worship House Media, http.worshiphousemedia.com/mini-movies/23285/Voices-Of-The-Cross.

2. How do you think these people might have responded to the idea that Jesus was raised from the dead?

3. How do people today respond to talk of Jesus' resurrection?

OPTION 2: SIGHTINGS

Say—

> Sometimes we might hear people talking about how they wished someone were alive again. Or they might say that so-and-so would turn over in their grave if they knew what was happening. And don't forget all the movies, books, and TV shows about vampires, the undead. Our culture seems to have a fascination with life after death. But how often do we really hear of someone claiming to see a person walking around who is known to have died?

Think of someone relevant to your group who is known to be dead but is often reported to be seen alive. A common example might be Elvis. Regardless of who you choose, continue with the following thoughts.

QUESTIONS TO ASK

1. What thoughts and emotions are usually expressed when people talk about this person?

2. How do people respond to the idea that this person was seen walking around town?

3. How do people today respond to talk of Jesus' resurrection?

TRANSITIONAL TRUTH

Say—

> We each need to decide for ourselves regardless of what anyone else thinks—is Jesus really raised from the dead? This is the most central question of our Christian faith. As Paul says in 1 Corinthians 15:17, "If Christ has not been raised, your faith is futile; you are still in your sins." Let's examine the evidences given for the resurrection.

HEARING THE WORD
(12-15 MINUTES)

FOUR VIEWS

Have the teens gather into at least four small groups. Give each teen a copy of the **Four Views worksheet** found at the end of this session and assign each group one reading. When most have finished, have each group share their findings as directed in the **Leader's worksheet**. You'll want to emphasize here that regardless of what was recorded or how things were explained, there is absolutely no debate about whether or not there was a body in the tomb. The question was never *Was there a body in the tomb?* but rather *Why is the body not in the tomb?*

TRANSITIONAL TRUTH

Say—

> Not only was the tomb empty, but Jesus himself appeared to Peter, and then to the twelve disciples. After that he appeared to

more than five hundred believers at the same time. Then he appeared to James, all the apostles, and Paul (see 1 Corinthians 15:5-8). Imagine what an experience that would have been to actually, physically see Jesus alive again! What did that mean for those people who saw him again? What does it mean for us today?

SHARING YOUR PERSPECTIVE
(15-20 MINUTES)

SIGNS OF LIFE

Have your teens stay in their small groups, and pass out a sheet of poster board and a box of markers for each group. Say something like—

> Paul's letter to the Romans gives us some incredible insight into what our lives should be like in light of Jesus being raised from the dead. I'm going to assign each group a short section from Romans, and I'd like each group to create a sign using pictures, symbols, words, or whatever you'd like to express what you think the Bible teaches about our life in Christ. Be sure also to look for the activity of each person of the Trinity—Father, Son, and Spirit—in the Bible passages to show how each is involved in our being raised to new life.

Assign the following passages to the groups:

- Romans 1:1-6
- Romans 5:1-11

- Romans 6:5-10
- Romans 8:9-17

When the time is up, have the groups share their posters and insights with the others.

TRANSITIONAL TRUTH

Say—

> So our triune God has revealed through the resurrection what it means to be restored in our relationship to God. On the cross, the Son was separated from the Father. At the resurrection, Jesus was restored to his place at the right hand of God where he intercedes for us (Romans 8:34). As believers we also are restored to a relationship with God that is absolutely incredible. Take in these amazing words from Romans 8:31-39 with me.

Read the passage with passion and confidence.

MAKING IT PERSONAL
(8-10 MINUTES)

LETTERS TO GOD

Start by saying something along these lines—

> As the Spirit-adopted children of the Father through Jesus Christ, we should experience a new life filled with hope because of the resurrection. To help personalize the resurrection in your life, I want each of you to write a letter as a child to your heavenly Father. Practice writing in light of who God

is—Father, Son, and Spirit. Share your joy in his love and your struggles with doubt. Open your heart to whatever God is teaching you, and commit to living in the power of the resurrection in your daily life. Lay everything at your Father's feet knowing that the Son is there to intercede for you and that the Spirit will guide you into all truth.

When you've finished writing, place your letter in an envelope. Seal the envelope, and address it to yourself at your home address. In a few weeks these will come to you as a reminder of what you've determined to do today.

Pass out letter-writing paper and envelopes to each teenager. Encourage them to find a quiet spot alone to think and write their letters. Instruct the teens to bring their sealed and addressed envelopes to you. (You'll be reminded to send out the letters at Session 11.) When you've collected letters from most or when the time is coming to a close, continue with the session.

BRINGING IT TOGETHER

Finish with something like—

We've only begun to look into the full meaning and power of the resurrection today. Let me encourage each of you to ask more questions and go deeper into this teaching. We'll continue in the sessions ahead to look into how our triune God works to see this new life come to reality in our lives. But let's finish today by praising the Father for the Spirit-empowered raising of the Son.

Pray something like this—

Praise be to you, the God and Father of our Lord Jesus Christ! In your great mercy, you have given us new birth into a living hope through the resurrection of Jesus from the dead by the power of the Holy Spirit. Please help us to live in the hope and power of that resurrection. Father, we ask this through your Son and in the power of the Spirit— one God, forever and ever. Amen.

SESSION 7:
EMPTY

FOUR VIEWS
SMALL-GROUP WORKSHEET

1. Read Matthew 27:57-28:15. How was Jesus buried? Why and how was Jesus guarded? How did the guards and priests respond to the resurrection? Was the body in the tomb?

2. Read Mark 15:42-16:8. How was Jesus buried? What was the women's concern as they started on their visit? What did they find when they arrived? Was the body in the tomb?

3. Read Luke 23:50-24:12. How was Jesus buried? What did the women see when they came with the spices? What did the two men say to them? How did the disciples respond to the news? Was the body in the tomb?

4. Read John 19:38-20:9. How was Jesus buried? What did Mary Magdalene do when she saw the tomb on the first day of the week? What did Peter and John find? Was the body in the tomb?

SESSION 7: EMPTY

FOUR VIEWS
LEADER'S WORKSHEET

1. Read Matthew 27:57-28:15. How was Jesus buried? Why and how was Jesus guarded? How did the guards and priests respond to the resurrection? Was the body in the tomb?

   The groups' findings should include the following: Jesus' body was buried in a rich man's tomb (Joseph of Arimathea). The body was wrapped in a linen cloth and placed in the tomb behind a large rolling stone. The religious leaders feared some deception by Jesus' followers to help Jesus look legitimate in his resurrection statements. So Pilate allowed a seal on the tomb and a royal guard to secure the place. After the resurrection, the priests paid the soldiers to spread a story that the disciples did, in fact, steal the body in spite of the efforts done to ensure this wouldn't happen. The body was not found in the tomb.

   After the teens have answered, say—

   Some people teach that Jesus' body was stolen by the disciples. According to this passage, how would you respond?[23]

2. Read Mark 15:42-16:8. How was Jesus buried? What was the women's concern as they started on their visit? What did they find when they arrived? Was the body in the tomb?

   The groups' findings should include the following: Pilate, surprised that Jesus was already dead, gave the body of Jesus to Joseph of Arimathea to be buried. The body was wrapped in linen cloth and placed in a tomb behind a rolling stone. The women were concerned that no one would be there with enough strength to roll the stone away for them to put spices upon the body. When they arrived they saw the stone rolled away and heard from a young man in white telling them to examine the spot and tell the disciples. The body was not found in the tomb.

[23.] For an excellent and concise treatment of these arguments against the resurrection, see Mark Driscoll and Gerry Breshears, *Doctrine: What Christians Should Believe* (Wheaton, Ill.: Crossway Books, 2010).

3. Read Luke 23:50-24:12. How was Jesus buried? What did the women see when they came with the spices? What did the two men say to them? How did the disciples respond to the news? Was the body in the tomb?

The groups' findings should include the following: The body was taken by Joseph of Arimathea, wrapped in linen cloth, and placed in a tomb behind a rolling stone. The women came and saw the stone rolled away and no body present. They also heard from two men who reminded them of Jesus' statement that he would be crucified and be raised again on the third day. When the women shared this with the disciples, the men did not believe them. Peter did run to check things out, but he couldn't explain what had happened. The body was not found in the tomb.

Note: This passage lists two men while Mark's account claims one and Matthew's declares there to be one angel. This does not need to be a contradiction. Rather, Matthew and Mark list only one of the two men or angels for their focus in recording the event.[24]

After the teens have answered, say—

Some people teach that the resurrection account is simply a hallucination of Jesus' followers. According to this passage, how would you respond?

4. Read John 19:38-20:9. How was Jesus buried? What did Mary Magdalene do when she saw the tomb on the first day of the week? What did Peter and John find? Was the body in the tomb?

The groups' findings should include the following: Jesus was buried by Joseph of Arimathea and Nicodemus. They wrapped the body in strips of linen along with spices in accordance with burial customs. The mixture for preparing the body for burial weighed about 75 pounds. They buried him in a new garden tomb. Mary Magdalene found the stone removed and told Peter she didn't know where the body had been moved. Peter and John came and found the linen and the burial cloth from Jesus' head folded nearby. The body was not found in the tomb.

After the teens have shared, say—

Some people teach that Jesus simply fainted on the cross and got himself out of the tomb later. According to this passage, how would you respond?

[24] J. Dwight Pentecost, *The Words and Works of Jesus Christ* (Grand Rapids, Mich.: Zondervan, 1981).

OVERVIEW

The focus of this session is being restored to a relationship with God. The teens will look at what the Bible teaches about being born again, understand what this means to them personally, and decide to live out their new lives in community with other believers.

SETTING THE TONE

Babies are dependent. Newborns can't walk to the car, much less drive to the grocery store or buy food or cook their own food—or even feed themselves. Thankfully newborns aren't born into isolation. We are born into families. When I was a child, my family surrounded me, loved me, fed me, taught me, and walked with me as I grew into a responsible adult. Now I have children of my own who can't seem to do anything on their own (surprise, surprise). So guess what I spend my time doing?

The Father offers us the opportunity through the Son to receive a new birth by the Spirit. We receive this gift through our personal decision, but we are not born again into isolation. God has seen fit for us to be born into a new family—his.

As teens grow in this understanding, they will come to see their responsibilities in God's family. You will find opportunities throughout this lesson to connect them to other members of the community of faith. Let me encourage you to choose at least one of those options. Teens need to be connected to the larger family of God. Teens will be taught, but they will also be teaching. They will be cared for, but they must also care for others. We are members of one another; we are family. As such, we reflect the close, family relationship modeled for us in the Trinity—Father, Son, Spirit. We can be eternally grateful to be called children of God.

BREAKING THE ICE
(7-8 MINUTES)

OPTION 1: LIFE WITH GOD

Say—

Now that we've seen what Jesus did and went through for us, let's remind ourselves why the Father sent his Son to do this.

Play the video *Life with God*. When it's finished, ask the group the following questions.

QUESTIONS TO ASK

1. **What has this video reminded you of?**
2. **What do you think a relationship with God looks like?**

25. *Life with God,* directed by Dan Stevers. Worship House Media, http.worshiphousemedia.com/mini-movies/13521/Life-With-God.

3. How do we receive this gift of new life and relationship with God?

OPTION 2: LIKE A CHILD

Plan ahead of time to have one or more young visitors at your gathering—ideally babies or toddlers. You'll also need parents or other leaders there to assist.

Say something like—

> When we are born, we aren't able to do much on our own. As we grow older, we tend to forget that we are still dependent on others. Maybe it would be good to go back a bit in time to think about what it's like to be a child.

Call the children in. You might even want to ask them a few fun questions about who takes care of them—as long as they're old enough to talk. While the kids are with you, ask your teens the following questions. You can decide if and when to dismiss the children during the discussion.

QUESTIONS TO ASK

1. How can you tell that these little ones are dependent?
2. How is this dependence the same or different from being a newborn child of God?
3. How do we receive this gift of new life and relationship with God?

TRANSITIONAL TRUTH

Continue with something like—

> God's mission is to restore fallen humanity to a relationship with himself. So the Father

sent the Son. And as John says, "to all who did receive him, to those who believed in his name, he gave the right to become children of God—children born not of natural descent, nor of human decision or a husband's will, but born of God" (John 1:12-13). Understanding just what it means to be born of God will be the focus of our next activity.

HEARING THE WORD
(15-20 MINUTES)

OPTION 1: ON BEING BORN . . . AGAIN

Have the teens get into small groups, and hand each one a copy of the **On Being Born . . . Again worksheet** found at the end of this session. You may want to assign one or two questions to each group to let them be more thorough in their answers. When most have finished, have teens share their answers with the large group.

OPTION 2: BEEN THERE—DONE THAT

Invite a pastor or elder at your church to come and talk about this concept of being born of God. You can give them a copy of the **On Being Born . . . Again worksheet** as a framework for their talk. It would be a great opportunity for sharing your church's perspective on this concept and how it plays out in personal and church life. The Sharing Your Perspective section that follows is intentionally flexible to accommodate timing for your speaker as well as question and answer from your teens.

TRANSITIONAL TRUTH

Say—

> As the apostle Paul realized his sinful condition, he exclaimed, "What a wretched man I am! Who will rescue me from this body that is subject to death? Thanks be to God, who delivers me through Jesus Christ our Lord!" (Romans 7:24-25). We each have access to the Father through the Son by the Spirit. It's one thing to know that in our heads but another thing altogether to experience that in relationship. Pastor Alistair Begg has said that "true faith means moving beyond the awareness of the existence of our Lord and Savior Jesus Christ to a living, personal relationship with Him."[26]

Let's consider our relationship with God for a few moments.

SHARING YOUR PERSPECTIVE
(15-18 MINUTES)

GOD'S STORY, MY STORY

You'll want to be prepared to follow up with any teen's questions or designate a person who your teens can go to for further counsel. Begin this time of sharing by saying something like—

> God has made a way for us to be part of his forever family. It's important to think about our story of being restored to a relationship

---

26. Alistair Begg, *What Angels Wish They Knew: The Basics of True Christianity* (Chicago, Ill.: Moody, 1999), 179.

with God. The Trinity is unified in their relationship with one another, and God has provided a way for us to be united with him. The story doesn't stop there though. We're also united to each other as members of God's family. With that in mind, we're going to take some time to share our stories with one another. You can share your earliest realization of your need for a Savior to rescue you from your sins. You should also tell us where you are now and how the Spirit is working in and through you, affirming that you are a member of God's family. If you don't know if you're part of God's family, listen closely as others share and feel free to ask any questions you might have. Our desire is for each of us to be able to say we have been born of God.

TRANSITIONAL TRUTH

Say—

As children of God we are brothers and sisters in the same forever family. With this, 1 John 3:11 tells us, "For this is the message you heard from the beginning: We should love one another." Knowing how much the Father loves us lets us know what it means to love. Knowing what the Son did for us shows us what it means to love. Knowing how the Spirit enables us gives us power to love others the way God loves us.

MAKING IT PERSONAL
(8-10 MINUTES)

Start with something like—

> **Writer and speaker Francis Chan has said, "The Holy Spirit is the one who fills believers with God's love and the one who enables us to love one another."[27] The Father has revealed his love to us through the Son, and the Spirit enables us to love one another with the Father's love. We might know this in our heads, but do we live it out in our daily lives? Let's think about some ways we can show God's love to the people around us—both our brothers and sisters and those who haven't been born into God's family yet.**

OPTION 1: SERVING IN LOVE

Prepare ahead of time some displays of various service opportunities in your church and community. You might ask for a few ministry leaders to be there to talk with your teens about each area.

Let the teens get up and look through some of the service opportunities at your church or in your community. If possible have some ministry leaders on hand to discuss options with your teens. The important concept here is to draw them to the idea of being a contributing member of God's family and sharing the love of Christ with others. Just as the Father, Son, and Spirit give wholly to each other and to us, we ought to reflect this wholehearted effort to love others. When you're ready, bring everyone back together to close in prayer.

YOU'LL NEED

- Ministry leaders from your church

- A display of service opportunities in your church or community

---

[27.] Francis Chan, *Forgotten God: Reversing Our Tragic Neglect of the Holy Spirit* (Colorado Springs, Colo.: David C. Cook, 2009), 95.

OPTION 2: PICTURES OF LOVE

Pass out paper and pens to your teens and have them to draw a grid on their sheet so they have four squares. Ask them to use basic words or images to show at least four ways they have experienced love in the family of God—or ways in which they could show love in God's family. When the time is up, ask a few teens to share their experiences.

BRINGING IT TOGETHER

Finish with something like—

> Jesus said, "By this everyone will know that you are my disciples, if you love one another" (John 13:35). When we are born again, we are not born into isolation. We are born into God's family. Let's pray as we pursue a life of love in the family of God.

Pray something like this—

> Our Father, thank you for the new life we have through your Son. Please help us to keep growing into one body through the Spirit and to show clearly the love we learn from you. May we live like brothers and sisters knowing that you're our Father. When other people look at us, may they see a love that draws them to a relationship with you and us. Father, we ask this through your Son and in the power of the Spirit—one God, forever and ever. Amen.

SESSION 8: FAMILY MATTERS

ON BEING BORN . . . AGAIN
SMALL-GROUP WORKSHEET

1. Read John 3:1-8. What does "born again" mean (or not mean)? Who is involved in this new birth? Can people be in a relationship with God without this birth? Why or why not?

2. Read John 14:15-21. Who does Jesus promise to send? Where will this person live? How does this person relate to the Father and the Son? When does this person come into someone's life?

3. Read Acts 2:29-39. What "cut to the heart" of the crowd? What does it mean to repent? What gift do we receive if we follow Peter's words?

4. Read 1 John 2:28-3:10. How do we know if we are "born of God" as his children? Will we be perfect? Why or why not? How does 1 John 1:8-10 relate?

5. Read Ephesians 2:11-22. How does it say we are brought near (v.13) or given access (v.18) to the Father? What was Jesus' purpose according to this passage? What are believers to be as a result?

SESSION 8: FAMILY MATTERS

ON BEING BORN . . . AGAIN
LEADER'S WORKSHEET

1. Read John 3:1-8. What does "born again" mean (or not mean)? Who is involved in this new birth? Can people be in a relationship with God without this birth? Why or why not?

   Born again is not being born to your biological mother. Instead it has to do with the work of the Holy Spirit "birthing" us into the family of God, giving us new spiritual life. There is a mystery to this work similar to hearing but not seeing the wind. No one can see the kingdom of God if he or she isn't born again.

2. Read John 14:15-21. Who does Jesus promise to send? Where will this person live? How does this person relate to the Father and the Son? When does this person come into someone's life?

   The Son will ask the Father to send another Advocate, the Spirit of truth. The Spirit was with the disciples then, but he would live inside individuals after Jesus went away. The Spirit seems to indicate a strong connection to the Son and the Father, so the believer comes to understand that God is in them. This passage doesn't indicate specifically, but twice it mentions those who obey what Jesus commands. The next passage will more clearly define this.

3. Read Acts 2:29-39. What "cut to the heart" of the crowd? What does it mean to repent? What gift do we receive if we follow Peter's words?

   This final portion of Peter's message deals with the death and resurrection of Jesus. The people were cut to the heart with the understanding that this Jesus was the one they had crucified. They had a personal responsibility for his death on the cross as we all do due to our sin.

   Repentance may be explained different ways. The word goes deeper than simply feeling sorry. It holds the meaning of "turning." Therefore, turning from our sin to God's view of the world in the name of Jesus Christ is what we do for the forgiveness of our sins. As a result the Holy Spirit is given to us. So the Spirit dwells in the believer at the time of repentance.

   Note: Baptism is closely associated with repentance, and you may want to speak with an elder from your church to best relay this teaching to your teens.

CREATIVE BIBLE LESSONS ON THE TRINITY

4. Read 1 John 2:28-3:10. How do we know if we are "born of God" as his children? Will we be perfect? Why or why not? How does 1 John 1:8-10 relate?

John indicates that those who do what is right have been born of God. Those who keep sinning do not live in God's family. This doesn't mean we'll be perfect people. John says that "what we will be has not yet been made known" (3:2). There is a progression to our being made perfect in Christ (see next session).

When God's children sin, John says they don't keep on or continue to sin. Instead they confess to the Father and turn from sinful ways.

5. Read Ephesians 2:11-22. How does it say we are brought near (v.13) or given access (v.18) to the Father? What was Jesus' purpose according to this passage? What are believers to be as a result?

We are brought near to the Father through the Son's shed blood, and we are given access to the Father through the Spirit. Jesus' purpose was to create in himself one person out of two—referring to bringing Jews and Gentiles together in one body through the cross. Whether Jew or Gentile, we all are granted access through the Spirit and are members of God's family. We are also the dwelling place in which God lives by his Spirit.

MORE THAN MEETS THE EYE

OVERVIEW

This lesson takes a different look at the transforming power of the Spirit. Teens will learn what the Bible teaches about transformation, understand its before and after effects, and examine where they are in their personal transformation.

SETTING THE TONE

Change is good. I'd like to change. I get frustrated with some of the things I do. Sometimes I feel like there's nothing I can do to keep from doing something royally stupid. After a series of foolish mistakes, I just want to stop running what seems to be an endless rat race and crawl into the nearest hole. Do you think your teens ever feel that way? Do you think they hear the high expectations of living the Christian life and think, *There's no way that I'm **not** going to mess this up*?

At times we don't take enough responsibility for our lives. Yet we also find ourselves not giving responsibility into better hands. Jesus said the Father would send the Holy Spirit to give us peace, so the power doesn't have to come from us. The Spirit will take what God has made in each of us and transform us into a powerhouse for his glory. That's what happened with the apostles. They were common men who were empowered to do uncommon things. They were uneducated in Scriptures but lived and preached God's Word in an incredible way. They were doubtful and fearful men who ended up standing boldly before the high-and-mighty to deliver a clear message about Jesus Christ.

As pastor Chuck Swindoll writes, "How can anyone explain the transformation? Was it some crash course they took, some upbeat seminar on leadership? No. Then maybe it was really the work of angels, but the disciples were given credit for it? No, the biblical record clearly states that it was the same group of once-timid men Jesus had trained. Perhaps some high-powered heavenly drug, some miracle-inducing chemical, was inserted into their bodies that changed the men overnight? Enough! There is only one intelligent answer: It was the arrival and the empowerment of the Holy Spirit."[28]

The Spirit has come, and he holds that same transforming power, the same power that raised Jesus Christ from the dead. This power lives inside all who believe in Jesus, and it's time for this power to be released.

BREAKING THE ICE
(8-10 MINUTES)

OPTION 1: THE ARRIVAL

Begin with something like—

Wouldn't it be cool if we could change into whatever we wanted? If we could simply

YOU'LL NEED

• A copy of the movie *Transformers*[29] and a way to play it

28. Charles Swindoll. *Flying Closer to the Flame: A Passion for the Holy Spirit* (Nashville, Tenn.: Word Publishing, 1993), 39.

29. *Transformers*, directed by Michael Bay (2007; Universal City, Calif., DreamWorks SKG: 2007, DreamWorks Video, DVD).

**imagine the way we want to look or the life
we'd like to have and somehow transform?
I wonder what that might look like.**

Play the clip from *Transformers* from the beginning of
scene 11 until Optimus Prime leans down to look at Sam
(approximately 1:02:51 on the DVD counter).

QUESTIONS TO ASK

1. **If you could change into something inanimate,
   what would it be—a car, palm tree, shoes?**
2. **When have you ever wished you could turn into
   something or someone else?**
3. **How do you think God would change your
   life right now if he decided to do something
   instantaneously?**

OPTION 2: EXPLOSIVE SITUATION

As you hold your two-liter bottle, begin by saying—

**You might think a person who believes in
God has a dull life—like a bottle of Diet
_____. It's kind of boring, you have
to admit. It's got all the good stuff taken
out of it! Sadly, a lot of Christians live that
way too—like they've got all the good stuff
taken out. What if there was something that
could change that? What if God intended
for your life to be filled with power so he
could be praised by the world because of
you? Wouldn't that be cool?**

> ## YOU'LL NEED
>
> • A two-liter bottle of *diet* soft
> drink
> • Mentos candy
> • A sharp knife
> • Rags or paper towels

At this point drop a Mentos in the bottle. Close the lid
and give it a shake. Now you can either toss it far away from
anyone else or puncture the bottle with something—just wear
something you don't mind getting sticky. Be prepared for
cleanup too.[30]

---

30. Please try this ahead of time. Illustrations like this can be a lot of fun, but they can also take away from
the purpose if things get out of hand. We'd rather illustrate the Holy Spirit's power than be standing in the
hospital praying for the Spirit's healing!

QUESTIONS TO ASK

1. What made the difference in the Diet _____?
2. How did the Mentos change what was inside this bottle?
3. How does the Holy Spirit relate to this little illustration?

TRANSITIONAL TRUTH

Say something like—

> So how can we be transformed? How do you get this power? People go about trying to get it in a variety of ways, but those ways stand in contrast to what Jesus taught his disciples. You may have heard of some of these great get-power-quick deals, but don't get your wallets out just yet.

SHARING YOUR PERSPECTIVE
(12-15 MINUTES)

POWERFUL ADVERTISING

Say—

> There are plenty of people willing to sell you something to help you get the look and feel you want. Maybe you've heard of the power of positive thinking. Or maybe you've heard people talk about how they could change if they could only get away from their family or get out of this town. Maybe people really get pumped up by a motivational speaker.

Let's see how those messages compare with what Jesus says in John 14.

Have the teens get into pairs, and give each pair a sheet of poster board and some markers. Have them draw an advertisement showing some of the ways people think they can be transformed. As they think through their plan, ask them to jot down a few verses from John 14 on the back that would support a more biblical understanding of transformation—verses that would answer the questions: Where's the power? Where's the focus? Give them seven or eight minutes to work on their ad. Then bring them back together to share their creations and insights about what they've learned.

TRANSITIONAL TRUTH

Say—

We all look for strength and power. People try to get it in lots of different ways, but there's only one place we can truly experience it—in a relationship with God. Jesus told his followers in Acts 1:8, "But you will receive power when the Holy Spirit comes on you." Power. Power to be a witness for Jesus. Power to live the way God tells us in his Word. Power to be transformed into a clearer likeness of Jesus. You don't have to have a lot of money. You don't have to be in a certain group. You don't have to amount to anything for the Spirit to empower you. Let's take a look at the lives of some men who experienced this kind of transformation.

HEARING THE WORD
(12-15 MINUTES)

YOU'LL NEED

• Copies of the **Before and After worksheet**

• Bibles

• Pens or pencils

BEFORE AND AFTER

Have the teens get into small groups; you can determine the number to fit your needs. Hand each one a copy of the **Before and After worksheet** found at the end of this session. Give each group time to answer the questions. You may want to assign one or two questions for each group to focus on more thoroughly. When most have finished, have each group share their answers with the large group.

TRANSITIONAL TRUTH

Say—

> You see, God doesn't just say "be different." He actually makes it happen as we realize and submit to the power of the Spirit. It's not something we have to do on our own. That's a freeing thought! Paul says, "Now the Lord is the Spirit, and where the Spirit of the Lord is, there is freedom. And we all, who with unveiled faces contemplate the Lord's glory, are being transformed into his image with ever-increasing glory, which comes from the Lord, who is the Spirit. (2 Corinthians 3:17-18) The Holy Spirit gets involved in every aspect of our life to bring about a new creation—a transformation—into something that looks an awful lot like Jesus.
>
> That kind of transformation can only be done with a supernatural power. We're

humans, so we're frail and unable to create an abundant life. "But we have this treasure in jars of clay to show that this all-surpassing power is from God and not from us" (2 Corinthians 4:7). The Holy Spirit is that treasure. He's that power inside our clay bodies that produces such a transformation. And the best part is—it brings glory to God, which is why we've been created. We're fulfilling our purpose simply by letting the Spirit transform our lives into the image of Jesus.

MAKING IT PERSONAL
(10-12 MINUTES)

Start by saying—

> What would this image look like? What are some qualities we might see or experience as a result of our transformation? Let's take some time to think and talk about it.

OPTION 1: A CHANGE IN THE PICTURE

Pass out drawing paper and markers to each teen. Have them draw a picture or two of how they think their lives would be different after a complete transformation by the power of the Holy Spirit. Ask them to share some of their drawings with the rest of the group.

YOU'LL NEED
- Paper
- Markers

OPTION 2: JARS OF CLAY

Pass out two or three index cards to each teen. As them to write words or short phrases to describe the transformed life. As they finish, have your teens drop their cards in the clay pot or jar you have in the room. When you've collected the

YOU'LL NEED
- A clay pot or jar
- Index cards
- Pens or pencils

cards, read a few out loud and ask for the group to discuss them further.[31]

BRINGING IT TOGETHER

Finish with something like—

> **We need to understand that the Holy Spirit empowers us to live life differently— transformed. The question you and I need to reflect on is, Am I allowing the Spirit to do this transformation? If we are, we should see fruit. If we are filled with the Spirit, we will see the Spirit pouring out of our lives to others in the unique ways we are gifted. It's not easy to become a new creation, but then, it's not about us. It's all about the Spirit. Let's pray and thank God for the presence of the Spirit and submit ourselves to his amazing power.**

Pray—

> **God, thank you for the example of Jesus and the transforming power of the Holy Spirit. Reveal to us anything that we still need to submit to you so we can be more conformed to the image of Christ. Father, we ask this through your Son and in the power of the Spirit—one God, forever and ever. Amen.**

PREPARATION NOTE

As a heads-up, check out the **Making It Personal** activity options for Session 12. You may want to review a few resources to order for your teens for that session. Or you might find the next discussion series you'll have when you've finished with this one.

[31.] The jar makes a nice visual in your room for the rest of the study. You can even take out a card or two before you begin future sessions to remind your teens of the transforming work of the Spirit. Or you can always use it for flowers, pencils, or whatever else you want to collect.

SESSION 9:
MORE THAN MEETS THE EYE

BEFORE AND AFTER
SMALL-GROUP WORKSHEET

Take some time to look at the lives of the apostles before the coming of the Holy Spirit in the Bible references found in the first column. Write down any ways your life might compare. Then go down the right column to see how the apostles' lives were transformed. Again write down any ways your life might relate.

BEFORE	AFTER
1. John 14:1	1. Acts 4:13
2. John 14:5	2. Acts 5:27-32
3. John 14:22	3. 1 Peter 4:12-13
4. Mark 14:66-72	4. Acts 5:41-42
5. Matthew 26:55-56	5. Acts 2:38-40

SESSION 9:
MORE THAN MEETS THE EYE

BEFORE AND AFTER
LEADER'S WORKSHEET

Take some time to look at the lives of the apostles before the coming of the Holy Spirit in the Bible references found in the first column. Write down any ways your life might compare. Then go down the right column to see how the apostles' lives were transformed. Again write down any ways your life might relate.

BEFORE	AFTER
1. John 14:1 *troubled*	1. Acts 4:13 *courageous*
2. John 14:5 *abandoned*	2. Acts 5:27-32 *confident in the Spirit's presence*
3. John 14:22 *loss of hope*	3. 1 Peter 4:12-13 *hope and joy in suffering*
4. Mark 14:66-72 *denial*	4. Acts 5:41-42 *perseverance*
5. Matthew 26:55-56 *left Christ*	5. Acts 2:38-40 *stood for Christ*

OVERVIEW

This session provides a discussion of how we develop godly character. Teens will take a look at the fruit of the Spirit, understand how fruit is grown in their lives, and choose to be involved with God in the growing process.

SETTING THE TONE

I don't have a green thumb. Actually, that's an understatement. I have the ability to kill any plant growing within 20 feet of me. I've tried to learn and be careful with how I water and care for plants, but every effort I make inevitably sucks the life out of every plant. My wife, however, can bring a struggling flower back to life. She has something like green *hands*. As any plant-lover would say, one can only watch for signs and set the stage for health and growth. The rest is up to nature. In our Christian worldview, we know the rest is up to God.

The fruit of the Spirit works much the same way. The Father has planted a vineyard where the Son is the Vine, and we are the branches. We look for signs of connectedness between our life and the Vine and place ourselves in the hands of our Father, the Vinedresser, for our health. In the process the Spirit feeds and empowers us to grow fruit—fruit reminiscent of the character of Christ. As writer Jerry Bridges puts it, "A life that grows in loving God becomes like God."[32] May we as leaders model a fruitful life on the Vine so our teens can experience the sweet life in community with God and others.

BREAKING THE ICE
(8-10 MINUTES)

YOU'LL NEED
- A bowl or bowls
- Assorted fruits

FRUIT BOWL

Be sure you have bowls with a variety of fruits set out ahead of time for this segment. Say something like—

> **Our new life in Christ should mean changes in our lives. With the Spirit growing inside us, we should begin to see the fruit of his work. As we talk about this today, let's take a few minutes to check out some tasty illustrations.**

Guide your teens through the following steps and questions.

32. Jerry Bridges, *The Fruitful Life: The Overflow of God's Love Through You* (Colorado Springs, Colo.: NavPress, 2006), 11.

QUESTIONS TO ASK

Let everyone choose a piece of fruit to eat about halfway through these questions.

1. **Take a look at the fruit. How would you describe them?**
2. **What's the difference between fresh and rotten fruit?**
   Note: Fresh fruit has recently been picked or harvested. Rotten fruit has been disconnected from its source for a long time and isn't fit to eat.
3. **What's the purpose of fruit?**
4. **What does healthy fruit depend upon? Hint: think about the tree or vine it grows on.**
5. **How do you think this relates to the Christian life?**

TRANSITIONAL TRUTH

Say—

> **When we come to the Father through the Son, the Spirit begins developing the character of Christ within us. That's why Peter says, "His divine power has given us everything we need for a godly life through our knowledge of him who called us by his own glory and goodness" (2 Peter 1:3). But what does that actually mean? How is the character of Christ formed in us? Let's answer these questions together.**

YOU'LL NEED

- Copies of the **Life on the Vine worksheet**
- Bibles
- Pens or pencils

HEARING THE WORD
(15-20 MINUTES)

LIFE ON THE VINE

Have the teens gather in small groups. Hand each one a copy of the **Life on the Vine worksheet** found at the end of this session. Give each group time to answer the questions. You may want to assign one or two questions for each group to focus on more thoroughly. When most have finished, have each group share their answers with the entire group.

TRANSITIONAL TRUTH

Say—

> **The fruit of the Spirit is the work of God in our lives, but we don't just sit back and watch it happen. As the Father, Son, and Spirit work together to grow fruit in our lives, we are to work with God in our character development. Philippians 2:12-13 says, "Therefore, my dear friends, as you have always obeyed—not only in my presence, but now much more in my absence—continue to work out your salvation with fear and trembling, for it is God who works in you to will and to act in order to fulfill his good purpose." We work; God works. With that in mind, let's take a closer look at the growth that is going on, positive and negative, on our branches.**

SHARING YOUR PERSPECTIVE
(10-12 MINUTES)

FRUIT LOOP

Pass out two copies of the **Fruit Loop worksheet** to each teenager; you'll find it at the end of this session. Say something like—

> We've already discussed the humility of Christ as well as the description of the fruit of the Spirit. Now it's time to evaluate each area to see how Christ is being formed in you.

Allow the teens time to work through this evaluation on their own. When most have finished, continue with the following questions.

QUESTIONS TO ASK

1. What stood out to you during your reflection?
2. How does growing fruit affect your relationship with our triune God? How does it affect your relationship with others?
3. Fruit is grown for giving and building up, so it's important for those we hope to "feed" to see our fruit. The second sheet is for you to take and give to a friend or family member. Ask them to evaluate you, and compare their thoughts with your own.

TRANSITIONAL TRUTH

Say something like—

> Our heavenly Father serves as the gardener who helps us as we grow spiritually.

YOU'LL NEED

- Copies of the **Fruit Loop worksheet**
- Bibles
- Pens or pencils

He both prunes and empowers us through Christ and the Spirit. As we work alongside him, we need to keep in mind both the things we're putting on—the fruit of the Spirit—as well as those things we should be putting off—sinful desires. Ephesians 4:22-24 says, "You were taught, with regard to your former way of life, to put off your old self, which is being corrupted by its deceitful desires; to be made new in the attitude of your minds; and to put on the new self, created to be like God in true righteousness and holiness." There is no neutral ground. We either grow in the sinful nature, or we grow in the Spirit. We either "grieve the Holy Spirit of God" (Ephesians 4:30) or we become "imitators of God" (Ephesians 5:1 NIV1984). Both have a tremendous effect on our relationships with God and with our brothers and sisters in God's family.

MAKING IT PERSONAL
(10-12 MINUTES)

THE VINE AND THE BRANCHES

Prepare ahead of time by drawing or cutting out a vine to display in your meeting room. You can write "Jesus Christ" on the vine. And you could also draw or create branches without leaves sprouting off the vine and labelled with the names of each of your teens.

Start by saying—

You've had a little bit of time to think about how you're growing fruit or not, and you've also considered some things that might be

YOU'LL NEED

- Large paper to draw or cut out a vine
- Construction paper
- Markers
- Tape
- A lawn bag or trash can

hindering or helping your growth. Take some green construction paper and cut out two or three leaves. On each leaf write something that might help or hinder you as you grow in the Spirit. Next take a colored sheet of paper and cut out a piece of fruit. On the fruit list one description from your Fruit Loop activity that you would like prayer about as you seek to grow in that area. When you've finished, stick your leaves and fruit on the branches of the vine.

When most of your teens have placed their leaves and fruit on the vine, have them pray for each another. Ask the teens to keep their eyes open as they pray. And as one prays for another, remove or prune any leaves that cause a hindrance and put them in a lawn bag or trash can.

BRINGING IT TOGETHER

Finish with something like—

Our love for our triune God will make all the difference in our fruit-growing. Ephesians 5:1-2 challenges us, "Be imitators of God, therefore, as dearly loved children and live a life of love, just as Christ loved us and gave himself up for us as a fragrant offering and sacrifice to God" (NIV1984). Let's commit our lives to God and each other now as we close in prayer.

Pray—

Father, thank you for loving us enough not only to nurture us but also to prune away things that keep us from being healthy. Please help us to remain in the Vine, Jesus your Son. May the Spirit feed and empower us to be more like Christ. Father, we ask this through your Son and in the power of the Spirit—one God, forever and ever. Amen.

PREPARATION NOTE

If you choose the option, don't forget to announce to your group that you'll be having a white elephant gift exchange next week. Set the price limit for the gifts, and tell your teens to bring their wrapped gifts for the session next week.

SESSION 10:
THE SWEET LIFE

LIFE ON THE VINE
SMALL-GROUP WORKSHEET

1. Read John 15:1-17, 26. How is the Father involved in the fruit-producing process? The Son? The Spirit? What should we do?

2. Read 2 Peter 1:3-9. How can we participate in the divine nature and abide in Christ? What is God's part in the process? What is our part in the process? What are the consequences of our decision?

3. Read Philippians 2:1-11. We read this before when we were discussing Christ's death. Now let's read it in light of his character. Was Jesus ever proud? How was he exalted? What attitude is presented here that we should have too (see verses 3-4 and 7-8)?

4. Read Galatians 5:16-26. How would you contrast the sinful nature from the divine nature (the Spirit)? What has been done by those who belong to Christ Jesus (v. 24)? What warning is given to believers as they cultivate the fruit of the Spirit?

SESSION 10:
THE SWEET LIFE

LIFE ON THE VINE
LEADER'S WORKSHEET

1. Read John 15:1-17, 26. How is the Father involved in the fruit-producing process? The Son? The Spirit? What should we do?
   The Father is the gardener or vinedresser. He cares for the vine and prunes the dead things off. The Son is the Vine, and we are the branches. The Son—the Vine—ensures that we will have everything we need to grow. The Spirit testifies to the truth of the Son and directs our attention to him. We should keep our attention on the fact that we must remain in the Son in order to remain fruitful.

2. Read 2 Peter 1:3-9. How can we participate in the divine nature and abide in Christ? What is God's part in the process? What is our part in the process? What are the consequences of our decision?
   We can participate through God's power and "precious promises." We can participate in and develop the divine nature of Christ. God provides his power, his Word, and "everything we need." We need to "make every effort" (v. 5) in cultivating the character of Christ as we work together with God. As we grow and progress, we'll be effective and fruitful. If we digress, we're blind and we forget the incredible work of Christ on our behalf.

3. Read Philippians 2:1-11. We read this before when we were discussing Christ's death. Now let's read it in light of his character. Was Jesus ever proud? How was he exalted? What attitude is presented here that we should have too (see verses 3-4 and 7-8)?
   Jesus never exhibited pride. He was exalted by God the Father. His attitude was one of humility, and we're told to model the same attitude (v. 5).

4. Read Galatians 5:16-26. How would you contrast the sinful nature from the divine nature (the Spirit)? What has been done by those who belong to Christ Jesus (v. 24)? What warning is given to believers as they cultivate the fruit of the Spirit?
   The sinful nature is contrary to the Spirit—they are in conflict with each other. There is no middle ground. You are participating in one or the other. The acts of the sinful nature are listed in verses 19-21. The fruit of the Spirit is listed in verses 22-23. This isn't a comprehensive list, but it serves as a great starting point. We're warned not to become proud in how fruitful we are or to envy other people's fruit. As already discussed in Question 3, humility is foundational.

SESSION 10:
THE SWEET LIFE

FRUIT LOOP
SMALL-GROUP WORKSHEET

Using the Bible verses and the loop below, color in or mark on each arrow to indicate how well each fruit of the Spirit is growing in your life right now. Connect the points around the circle to show how well balanced your life is. Then think about what might be hindering or helping these fruits grow in your life. Remember: none of us has arrived yet. Even the apostle Paul said, "Not that I have already obtained all this, or have already arrived at my goal, but I press on to take hold of that for which Christ Jesus took hold of me" (Philippians 3:12).

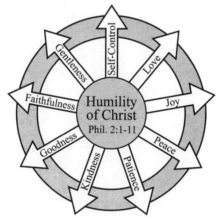

Use these Bible verses to evaluate the fruit in your life:

Love: 1 Corinthians 13:4-7; 1 John 4:19-21
Joy: Philippians 4:4; 1 Thessalonians 5:16
Peace: John 16:33; Romans 12:18
Patience: Ephesians 4:2; Colossians 3:12-13
Kindness: Luke 6:35-36; Titus 3:3-7
Goodness: Galatians 6:10; Ephesians 2:8-10
Faithfulness: Proverbs 20:6; Luke 16:10
Gentleness: Isaiah 40:11; Colossians 3:12
Self-Control: Proverbs 25:28; 1 Thessalonians 4:3-8
Humility: Philippians 2:1-11; James 4:10

OVERVIEW

This session focuses on the gifts of the Spirit. Teens will consider what spiritual gifts are, understand how and why we receive them, and choose to use their gifts in service to God and others.

SETTING THE TONE

Sometimes we are thrilled beyond words when we receive gifts. Other times we think, *What were they thinking?* Some gifts come about naturally. Others need a rather bulky instruction manual. To some extent we could say some of the same things about gifts we have received from God. Yet we can trust that the Father knows what he's doing—Jesus proved that.

The Holy Spirit is the person of the Godhead who fills us with God's gifts, and the gifts of the Spirit are not simply dropped into our lives for us to figure out on our own. God works in and through us to make those gifts known as well as useful for his purposes. As your teens will see, some gifts may seem more desirable than others, but God gives them all for the building up of his family. It's not about the individual gift or even the individual person—it's about the service, the love, the community, the *missio dei* (mission of God, Session 3). Let's pray that our teens begin to recognize their giftedness and allow God to make use of those gifts for his glory.

BREAKING THE ICE
(18-20 MINUTES)

YOU'LL NEED

- A few extra gifts
- A bowl
- Numbered papers for a drawing

OPTION 1: WHITE ELEPHANT GIFT EXCHANGE

Be sure to announce ahead of time that this is happening. A reminder is listed for you in Session 10, but you may want to give even more advance notice. Plan also to bring a few wrapped gifts for any visitors you might have or for those who forget. You'll also need to prepare ahead a bowl with numbered papers inside for teens to draw the order they'll choose gifts. If you have a large group, simply break down to smaller groups of about 10 people. Of course, you'll need multiple bowls for drawing numbers, but smaller groups will help keep you closer to the suggested timing for the session.

Say—

> Everyone likes to receive gifts, so we're going to exchange gifts today. Everyone should choose a number from the bowl, and we'll go in that order. The first person will pick a gift and open it. The following people

can choose a gift previously opened or take a new one. At the end, the first person will be able to choose any gift they like or keep the one they have.

When everyone has finished, ask the following questions.

QUESTIONS TO ASK

1. Do you like getting gifts this way? Why or why not?
2. How do you think this is like or unlike the way we receive gifts from God?

OPTION 2: BIRTHDAY MEMORIES

Be sure to bring in a birthday cake complete with candles. You might also want to decorate and give party hats or favors to each teen. Designate someone as the recipient of this birthday party.

YOU'LL NEED

- Birthday cake
- Candles
- Other party supplies

Say something like—

> Birthday parties almost always bring up memories—some good, some not so good. We're going to go around and have everyone share a good or bad memory from a previous birthday.

When the teens have finished sharing, ask the following questions if they haven't already come up during the discussion.

QUESTIONS TO ASK

1. What was your favorite gift that you received for a birthday? Why?
2. Do you think God gives good gifts? Why or why not?

TRANSITIONAL TRUTH

Say—

> We don't usually try to give bad gifts. We want to give a person something she will enjoy. Sometimes we get it right; sometimes we don't.
>
> God also gives us gifts, and his gifts are always good. James 1:17 tells us that "every good and perfect gift is from above, coming down from the Father of the heavenly lights, who does not change like shifting shadows."
>
> If God gives us each good gifts, how do we get them? When we repent and believe in the Son, the Father sends us the Spirit as a gift. Jesus said in Luke 11:13, "If you then, though you are evil, know how to give good gifts to your children, how much more will your Father in heaven give the Holy Spirit to those who ask him!" The Spirit is the person of the Trinity who gives us special gifts to be used to serve God and others. Let's take a closer look at how this plays out.

HEARING THE WORD
(12-15 MINUTES)

GIFT LIST

Before you begin, you'll want to be prepared to relay your church's viewpoint on what some call "sign gifts," including miraculous powers and speaking in tongues. If you're unsure, ask a pastor or elder to join your group or provide information to help you prepare.

Have the teens get into small groups; you can decide how many. Hand each one a copy of the **Gift List worksheet** found at the end of this session, and give each group time to answer the questions. You may want to assign one or two questions to each group so they can answer more thoroughly. When most have finished, have each group share their answers with the large group.

TRANSITIONAL TRUTH

Continue with something like—

> First Corinthians 12:20-27 says, "As it is, there are many parts, but one body. The eye cannot say to the hand, 'I don't need you!' And the head cannot say to the feet, 'I don't need you!' On the contrary, those parts of the body that seem to be weaker are indispensible, and the parts that we think are less honorable we treat with special honor. And the parts that are unpresentable are treated with special modesty, while our presentable parts need no special treatment. But God has put the body together, giving greater honor to the parts that lacked it, so that there should be no division in the body, but that its parts should have equal concern for each other. If one part suffers, every part suffers with it; if one part is honored, every part rejoices with is. Now you are the body of Christ, and each one of you is a part of it."
>
> With that in mind, let's practice what it's like to work together as one body.

SHARING YOUR PERSPECTIVE
(7-8 MINUTES)

COORDINATED EATING

Prepare by setting out bowls full of messy food, such as pudding, along with spoons. You'll also want some old shirts or towels to give to the person being fed.

Select several trios of participants for this activity. One person should wear the towel and sit in front of the bowl of pudding. Another should be blindfolded and will be the one doing the feeding. The third will be the eyes and mouth of the operation, giving guidance and trying to help the pudding get eaten.

Say something like—

> **We need our body to work together every single time we sit down for a meal. But this activity will show us the difficulties in bringing the body together.**

Set a time limit, and let the teams go at it. Be prepared to award a prize to the group that wins—perhaps some pudding!

QUESTIONS TO ASK

1. **How did the competition go? What were some of the successes? What were some of the difficulties?**
2. **Have you seen some similar successes and difficulties in the church? Explain.**
3. **Who helps us function as a healthy body that reflects the perfectly functioning Trinity?**

YOU'LL NEED

- Pudding or other messy food
- Bowls
- Spoons
- Towels or old T-shirts
- Blindfolds

TRANSITIONAL TRUTH

Say something like—

> In our game one person couldn't be fed
> without the help of others. That's the way
> things work here in our church and com-
> munity. Some people need our help in order
> to do their part in the body. Galatians 5:13-
> 14 says, "You, my brothers and sisters, were
> called to be free. But do not use your free-
> dom to indulge the flesh; rather, serve one
> another humbly in love. For the entire law
> is fulfilled in keeping this one command:
> 'Love your neighbor as yourself.'" Our gifts
> aren't for our personal enjoyment. We are
> meant to use them to serve and love others
> and to bring praise to God.

MAKING IT PERSONAL
(10-12 MINUTES)

OPTION 1: GIVING THE LOVE

Divide your teens into smaller groups, and pass out poster
board and markers to each group. Say—

> Think through the gifts represented in each
> of your groups. Share what you think some
> of your spiritual gifts might be, and brain-
> storm about how your group could work
> together to serve others in our church and
> community in the next month. Write your
> ideas along with some plans that could be
> the foundation for a service project that we
> can do in our larger group or in our smaller

YOU'LL NEED

- Poster board
- Markers

groups to share the love of Christ with others.

When time is up have the groups share their ideas with the others.

OPTION 2: BE THE CHANGE

Say something like—

> You might not think you're in a place to make a difference right now, but you might need to think again. Let's take a look at a testimony from one teen who decided to use his gifts to share the love of Christ.

Play the video *Zach Hunter on Be the Change.* When the video is over ask the following questions.

QUESTIONS TO ASK

1. What gifts did Zach use to share the love of Christ with others?
2. How would you describe his mission? How does it relate to God's mission?
3. What are some ways you can begin to use your gifts and passion to serve others?

BRINGING IT TOGETHER

Finish with something like—

> Our triune God works together to guide and empower us to bring him glory and share his love with others. Let's keep each other accountable to be humble with whatever gifts we've been given. Let's remember that our gifts aren't for our personal benefit. Our gifts are how God works through

33. *Zach Hunter on Be the Change,* Zondervan Publishers, www.godtube.com/watch/?v=6DZLNNNX.

us to build up his family and to share his heart with the world. Let's pray together and commit to using our giftedness for God's purposes.

Pray—

Father, we know that every good and perfect gift comes from you. Thank you that your Son has made a way to you and stands with you to send your Spirit into us. May your Spirit reveal our gifts to us so we can cultivate and use them to bring you praise and to share your heart with other people. Father, we ask this through your Son and in the power of the Spirit—one God, forever and ever. Amen.

PREPARATION NOTE

Don't forget this week to mail out the **Letters to God** from Session 7. You'll discuss them in your group next week.

SESSION 11:
HAPPY BIRTHDAY!

GIFT LIST
SMALL-GROUP WORKSHEET

1. Read 1 Corinthians 12:1-11. How do we receive these gifts? What are some of the gifts listed here? Which ones resonate with you? What remains the same in all of these different gifts?

2. Read Ephesians 4:1-16. Why are we given these gifts from God (vv. 12-16)? What are some of the gifts listed here? Which ones resonate with you? What brings everyone together in unity despite all the diversity?

3. Read Romans 12:3-8. How are we to serve God and others with these gifts? What are some of the gifts listed here? Which ones resonate with you? How do all these body parts come together?

4. Read 1 Peter 4:7-11. Why does Peter tell us we need to act urgently? What should we keep in mind as our source and strength when we use our gifts? What are the two areas of focus for using our gifts?

SESSION 11:
HAPPY BIRTHDAY!

GIFT LIST
LEADER'S WORKSHEET

1. Read 1 Corinthians 12:1-11. How do we receive these gifts? What are some of the gifts listed here? Which ones resonate with you? What remains the same in all of these different gifts?

   The Spirit gives these gifts on behalf of the Father to each one as he determines (see also James 1:17). The gifts include wisdom, knowledge, faith, healing, miraculous powers, prophecy, distinguishing between spirits, speaking in tongues, and interpretation of tongues. Teens will share which ones they might see in their own lives. What remains the same is the same Spirit.

   NOTE: Make sure you're prepared to relay your church's viewpoint on what some call "sign gifts," including miraculous powers and speaking in tongues. If you're unsure, ask a pastor or elder to join your group or provide information to help you prepare.

2. Read Ephesians 4:1-16. Why are we given these gifts from God (vv. 12-16)? What are some of the gifts listed here? Which ones resonate with you? What brings everyone together in unity despite all the diversity?

   To prepare God's people to serve him and to build up others in his family until we are all mature in Jesus Christ. The gifts listed here are apostleship, prophecy, evangelism, and pastoring-teaching. Teens will share which ones they might see in their own lives. What brings us together in unity is the one Spirit, one Father, one Lord (Son), one faith, one baptism.

3. Read Romans 12:3-8. How are we to serve God and others with these gifts? What are some of the gifts listed here? Which ones resonate with you? How do all these body parts come together?

   We are to serve in humility. Remind teens of Session 10 and the foundation of our fruit. We are to use our gifts without holding back—generously, diligently, and cheerfully. The gifts listed are prophecy, service, teaching, encouragement, contributing (giving), leadership, and showing mercy. Teens will share which ones they might see in their own lives. We all are one in Christ.

4. Read 1 Peter 4:7-11. Why does Peter tell us we need to act urgently? What should we keep in mind as our source and strength when we use our gifts? What are the two areas of focus for using our gifts?

The end of all things is near. In other words, Jesus is coming soon, and we need to act now! We should speak as if our words are the very words of God and serve in God's strength. The two areas of focus are others (v. 10) and God (v. 11).

OVERVIEW

This session encourages teens to be on God's mission. Teens will see how the Trinity reveals God's heart for the world, understand that they are fellow workers with God, and commit to joining God's mission.

SETTING THE TONE

For most of my life, I thought my faith was only about me. I was taught to have a *personal* relationship with Jesus, to make sure I had a *personal* quiet time, and to reflect on my *personal* growth in Christ. Everything guided me to think that God's mission was all about me. It only made sense that I had to work through struggles on my own— they were my *personal* struggles.

After studying God's Word for some time now, I've realized just how deadly that thinking is. If we have learned anything in our study of the Trinity, we should know that the very nature of the Trinity is relational. God's mission in the world is about relationship, but it's not just about me. God's heart is that every nation, tribe, language, and people hear and have opportunity to respond to his offer of restored relationship with himself (Revelation 5:9; 14:6). Pastor Tony Evans has said that "knowing who he is defines who we are."[34] If God has relationship within himself and is on a mission to restore relationship with humanity, then we should function within a relational community and be on a mission to see others restored to relationship with God.

What better time to understand and go on a mission with God than during the teen years? Proverbs 20:29 says, "The glory of young men is their strength." In the words of Alex and Brett Harris, "At no other time are we better positioned to decide who we will become . . . we can choose to set direction, develop character, and build momentum for an amazing future."[35] I can't imagine a future more amazing than one filled with restored relationships and bringing honor and glory to the God who is three in one! May this session serve as a type of commissioning service as your teens go on God's mission.

BREAKING THE ICE
(8-10 MINUTES)

Begin your session with something like—

> **Today we'll take all we have learned about our triune God and make a choice. Will it all be talk, or will we translate our knowledge into action? We are the light of the world—the question is, what kind of light**

34. Tony Evans, *Our God Is Awesome* (Chicago, Ill.: Moody Publishers, 1994), p. 17.

35. Alex and Brett Harris, *Do Hard Things* (Colorado Springs, Colo.: Multnomah Books, 2008), p. 50.

are we? There are people of every nation, tribe, and language who are still in desperate need of a relationship with our great God. Let's make our time today be the beginning or continuation of our going on God's mission.

OPTION 1: YOUR CITY WAITS

Play the video *Your City Waits*. Then ask your group the following questions.

QUESTIONS TO ASK

1. What pains of the people in the city are listed? Are these relational pains? Why or why not?
2. How does the video describe us as being able to reach the people?
3. God is a Trinity. He exists in eternal relationship with himself, and his mission is to restore relationship with humanity. How are we part of that mission?

OPTION 2: BEGINNING AT THE END

Read all of Revelation 5. Then ask the following questions.

QUESTIONS TO ASK

1. Who was worthy to open the scroll? What made him worthy?
2. Describe the people who were brought into God's kingdom as a result of this mission? (Check out verse 9.)
3. God is a Trinity. He exists in eternal relationship with himself, and his mission is to restore relationship with humanity. How are we part of that mission?

---

36. *Your City Waits,* directed by Fresh Purpose Productions, Worship House Media, http.worshiphousemedia. com/mini-movies/20417/Your-City-Waits.

TRANSITIONAL TRUTH

Say—

> The Father spoke and revealed himself
> through the Son and the Spirit. His mis-
> sion is clearly seen through the Son's obe-
> dience. And his mission continues through
> the work of the Spirit. But God has chosen
> to use us to represent him to the world. We
> should know who he is so we can represent
> him clearly to those around us. That's why
> we've been studying the Trinity. Let's take
> a few minutes to review what we know as we
> seek to go on a mission with God.

HEARING THE WORD
(8-10 MINUTES)

YOU'LL NEED

• Copies of *The Apostles'
Creed*

OPTION 1: THE APOSTLES' CREED

Use the reading sheet for The Apostles' Creed found at the
end of this session. You might read one line and then have
the teens repeat after you, or you might want to make enough
copies for everyone in the room to read in unison.

Say something like—

> The universal church (sometimes called
> catholic in some versions of the Apostles'
> Creed but not to be confused with the Roman
> Catholic Church) has worked for centuries
> on a clear understanding of the Trinity. The
> best known result is a description called the
> Apostles' Creed. Let's read it together.

When you finish, ask the following questions.

QUESTIONS TO ASK

1. Do you agree with this statement of faith? Why or why not?
2. How does this statement reflect what we know about God being three in one?
3. Does this statement of faith reveal the heart of God for the world?
4. Is it simply enough for us to believe this? Why or why not?

OPTION 2: THE GREAT COMMISSION

Say something like—

> Jesus talked about what we now call the Great Commission before he ascended into heaven. It wasn't a statement only for the disciples present at that time; it applies to everyone who chooses to follow Christ. Let's listen and reflect on these words together.

Read Matthew 28:18-20. You might read one line and then have the teens repeat after you, or you might encourage your teens to look it up and read it together. When you finish, ask the following questions.

QUESTIONS TO ASK

1. Does Jesus present this as a suggestion or a command? Explain.
2. How does this passage reflect what we know about God being three in one?
3. Does this passage reveal the heart of God for the world?
4. Is it enough for us simply to read this? Why or why not?

YOU'LL NEED

• Bibles

TRANSITIONAL TRUTH

Continue—

> God hasn't simply called us to know him. He has called us to make him known. We might have faith, but the world won't be restored to relationship with God without action. James 2:14-17 says, "What good is it, my brothers and sisters, if someone claims to have faith but has no deeds? Can such faith save them? Suppose a brother or sister is without clothes and daily food. If one of you says to them, 'Go in peace; keep warm and well fed,' but does nothing about their physical needs, what good is it? In the same way, faith by itself, if it is not accompanied by action, is dead."
>
> Let's take a look back and reflect on how this knowledge of the Trinity has changed our view of God, ourselves, and others.

SHARING YOUR PERSPECTIVE
(12-15 MINUTES)

A LIVING FAITH

If you have a large group, you may want to divide into smaller groups to go through this activity together. It will be important to give every teen a voice. When it seems that everyone has spoken, continue with the session.

Say—

> We're going to have everyone share what we've learned and how we've grown during our study together. You should have received your letter to God in the mail this week, and you might want to use that to decide what you want to say. But let's all share something about how our view of God, ourselves, and others has changed—or not changed—during this study.

TRANSITIONAL TRUTH

Continue with something like—

> May God be praised by all we have shared here together. It's good to be in relationship with God and be part of his family. We need to continue to "spur one another on toward love and good deeds" (Hebrews 10:24), especially because we know Jesus will one day return and there are still many people who aren't part of God's family.

MAKING IT PERSONAL
(15-20 MINUTES)

Regardless of which option you choose here, you might consider providing a copy of the books *Do Hard Things* by Alex and Brett Harris[37] or *Be the Change* by Zach Hunter.[38] Both are great resources by teenage authors to spur your teens on to love and good deeds.

[37.] Alex and Brett Harris, *Do Hard Things* (Colorado Springs, Colo.: Multnomah Books, 2008).

[38.] Zach Hunter, *Be the Change: Your Guide to Freeing Slaves and Changing the World,* (Grand Rapids, Mich.: Youth Specialties/Zondervan, 2007).

YOU'LL NEED

• The video **Know the Word: Lose Your Life**[39] (available at *www.worshiphousemedia. com* and a way to play it

OPTION 1: LIVE THE WORD

Say—

> Sometimes we get so caught up in how our world says life ought to be that we don't see how being on God's mission relates. Let's watch how one teen wrestles with this, and we can begin to work through ways we might respond to God's call.

Play the video *Know the Word: Lose Your Life*. Then continue with the following questions.

QUESTIONS TO ASK

1. Do you think this teen's response is extreme or irresponsible? Why or why not?
2. How would you describe his driving desire and motivation?

Continue with something like—

> Let's share some ways that each of us can begin to take seriously the Great Commission. You can speak for yourself, our group, or others in our group as you recognize the gifts and abilities God has given each of us to function as his body.
>
> Give the teens some time to brainstorm. You might even give an example by mentioning a way for one of your teens to use his or her giftedness for God's mission. Encourage teens to speak into each other's lives and think more in terms of community than individual pursuits. Some might even reference the service project from the last session—that's a great way to motivate

---

[39.] *Know the Word: Lose Your Life,* directed by Student Life, Worship House Media, www.worshiphousemedia.com/mini-movies/14607/Know-The-Word-Lose-Your-Life.

the group toward action and not only talk. Move on with the session when you're ready.

OPTION 2: DO HARD THINGS

Say—

> Sometimes we buy into the idea that teenagers can't do much. But this is not the way God views us. A couple of teens named Alex and Brett Harris learned that and shared some of their insights in a book. Let me read some of it for you.

Read the section "What the Bible Says About Teens" in Chapter 3 of *Do Hard Things*. When you've finished, ask the following questions.

QUESTIONS TO ASK

1. What thoughts or feelings came to you as you listened?
2. What big things are you passionate about but feel that you can't do anything to make a difference?
3. How do your passions and ideas line up with God's mission?

BRINGING IT TOGETHER

Finish with something like—

> The God who is three in one has spoken and revealed his desire to have a relationship with us, and he initiated a plan to make that happen. God himself miraculously came to earth in order to live as a perfect human, die in our place, and be raised from the dead to give us hope that we can be part of his family. As he works in our lives, we

---

40. Alex and Brett Harris, *Do Hard Things*.

are changed more and more into his image. We begin to look like him and live like him and represent his heart and mission for the world. God did it all so the world could come to know the one true God who is the Trinity. Let's think big and be committed to be on mission with the Father in the power of the Spirit until the Son returns.

Pray something like this—

God, thank you that we can live in relationship with you and with each other as members of your family. May we constantly be in your Word, Father, so we might know and understand your heart for the world. May we keep your Son ever before us as an example of an obedient life. May your Spirit empower us to take your message of love to the world. Father, we ask this through your Son and in the power of the Spirit—one God, forever and ever. Amen.

SESSION 12:
GO WITH GOD

THE APOSTLES' CREED
READING SHEET

I believe in God, the Father almighty,
creator of heaven and earth.
I believe in Jesus Christ, his only Son, our Lord,
who was conceived by the power of the Holy Spirit,
born of the virgin Mary,
suffered under Pontius Pilate,
was crucified, died, and was buried;
he descended to the dead.
On the third day he rose again,
he ascended into heaven,
is seated at the right hand of the Father
and will come again to judge the living and the dead.
I believe in the Holy Spirit,
the holy universal church,
the communion of saints,
the forgiveness of sins,
the resurrection of the body,
and the life everlasting.
Amen.

BIBLIOGRAPHY

Begg, Alistair. *What Angels Wish They Knew: The Basics of True Christianity.* Chicago, Ill.: Moody, 1999.

Bridges, Jerry. *The Fruitful Life: The Overflow of God's Love Through You.* Colorado Springs, Colo.: NavPress, 2006.

Chan, Francis. *Forgotten God: Reversing Our Tragic Neglect of the Holy Spirit.* Colorado Springs, Colo.: David C. Cook, 2009.

Driscoll, Mark and Breshears, Gerry. *Doctrine: What Christians Should Believe.* Wheaton, Ill.: Crossway Books, 2010.

Evans, Tony. *Our God Is Awesome.* Chicago, Ill.: Moody Publishers, 1994.

Gromacki, Robert. *The Holy Spirit: Who He Is, What He Does.* Word Publishing, 1999.

Grudem, Wayne. *Systematic Theology: An Introduction to Biblical Doctrine.* Grand Rapids, Mich.: Zondervan, 1994.

Harris, Alex and Brett. *Do Hard Things.* Colorado Springs, Colo.: Multnomah Books, 2008.

Hengel, Martin. *Crucifixion in the Ancient World and the Folly of the Message of the Cross.* Philadelphia, Pa.: Fortress Press, 1977.

Hunter, Zach. *Be the Change: Your Guide to Freeing Slaves and Changing the World.* Grand Rapids, Mich.: Youth Specialties/Zondervan, 2007.

James, Steven, *Never the Same*. El Cajon, Calif.: Youth Specialties, 2005.

Jeremiah, David. *God in You: Releasing the Power of the Holy Spirit in Your Life*. Multnomah, 1998.

Köstenberger, Andreas, and Swain, Scott. *Father, Son and Spirit: The Trinity and John's Gospel*. Downers Grove, Ill.: IVP Academic, 2008.

LeFever, Marlene. *Learning Styles: Reaching Everyone God Gave You to Teach*. Colorado Springs, Colo.: David C. Cook Publishing Co., 1995.

McFarland, Alex. *Stand: Core Truths You Must Know for an Unshakable Faith*. Carol Stream, Ill.: Tyndale House, 2005.

McGrath, Alister E. *Understanding the Trinity*. England: Kingsway Publications, Ltd., 1988.

J. Dwight Pentecost. *The Words and Works of Jesus Christ*. Grand Rapids, Mich.: Zondervan, 1981.

Robbins, Maggie and Robbins, Duffy. *Enjoy the Silence*. Grand Rapids, Mich.: Youth Specialties, 2005.

Sanders, Fred and Issler, Klaus. *Jesus in Trinitarian Perspective: An Introductory Christology*. Nashville, Tenn.: B&H Publishing, 2007.

Swindoll, Charles R. *Flying Closer to the Flame: A Passion for the Holy Spirit*. Nashville, Tenn.: Word Publishing, 1993.

Ware, Bruce A. *Father, Son, and Holy Spirit: Relationships, Roles, and Relevance*. Wheaton, Ill.: Crossway Books, 2005.

CREATIVE BIBLE LESSONS

The best-selling Creative Bible Lessons series will give you insightful, creative, and fun ways to teach your students more about the stories of God and His people.

Creative Bible Lessons in Essential Theology
Andrew Hedges
ISBN 978-0-310-86719-7

Creative Bible Lessons on the Trinity
Andrew Hedges
ISBN 978-0-310-67119-0

Creative Bible Lessons in Romans
Chap Clark
ISBN 978-0-310-20777-1

Creative Bible Lessons from the Old Testament
Laurie Polich
ISBN 978-0-310-22441-9

Creative Bible Lessons in 1 & 2 Corinthians
Marv Penner
ISBN 978-0-310-23094-6

Creative Bible Lessons in Galatians and Philippians
Tim McLaughlin, J. Cheri McLaughlin, Jim Miller, Yolanda Miller
ISBN 978-0-310-23177-6

Creative Bible Lessons in Psalms
TIm Baker
ISBN 978-0-310-23178-3

Creative Bible Lessons on the Prophets
Crystal Kirgiss
ISBN 978-0-310-24137-9

Creative Bible Lessons in Revelation
Randy Southern
ISBN 978-0-310-25108-8

Creative Bible Lessons in 1 & 2 Timothy and Titus
Len Evans
ISBN 978-0-310-25528-4

Creative Bible Lessons in John
Jay Ashcraft, Janice Ashcraft
ISBN 978-0-310-20769-6

Creative Bible Lessons in Nehemiah
Andrew Hedges
ISBN 978-0-310-25880-3

Creative Bible Lessons from the Life of Christ
Doug Fields
ISBN 978-0-310-40251-0

Creative Bible Lessons in Ezekiel
Anna Aven Howard
ISBN 978-0-310-26960-1

Creative Bible Lessons in Job
Doug Ranck
ISBN 978-0-310-27219-9

Creative Bible Lessons in Genesis
Hoon Kim
ISBN 978-0-310-27093-5

youth specialties

Share Your Thoughts

With the Author: Your comments will be forwarded to the author when you send them to *zauthor@zondervan.com*.

With Zondervan: Submit your review of this book by writing to *zreview@zondervan.com*.

Free Online Resources at
www.zondervan.com

Zondervan AuthorTracker: Be notified whenever your favorite authors publish new books, go on tour, or post an update about what's happening in their lives at www.zondervan.com/authortracker.

Daily Bible Verses and Devotions: Enrich your life with daily Bible verses or devotions that help you start every morning focused on God. Visit www.zondervan.com/newsletters.

Free Email Publications: Sign up for newsletters on Christian living, academic resources, church ministry, fiction, children's resources, and more. Visit www.zondervan.com/newsletters.

Zondervan Bible Search: Find and compare Bible passages in a variety of translations at www.zondervanbiblesearch.com.

Other Benefits: Register to receive online benefits like coupons and special offers, or to participate in research.

ZONDERVAN®

ZONDERVAN.com/
AUTHORTRACKER
follow your favorite authors